Positively
Cath[]lic

MICHAEL LEACH

Positively

Cath+lic

25 REALLY GOOD REASONS

to Love the Faith, Live the Faith, and Share the Faith

LOYOLAPRESS.
A JESUIT MINISTRY

Chicago

LOYOLA PRESS.
A JESUIT MINISTRY

3441 N. Ashland Avenue
Chicago, Illinois 60657
(800) 621-1008
www.loyolapress.com

This material first appeared in *Why Stay Catholic? Unexpected Answers to a Life-Changing Question* by Michael Leach (Loyola Press, 2011).

Cover design by Jill Arena
Interior design by Donna Antkowiak
Cover art credit: © iStock/Zack Blanton
Author photo credit back cover: Gregory A. Shemitz

ISBN-13: 978-0-8294-4491-9
ISBN-10: 0-8294-4491-2
Library of Congress Control Number: 2016941414

Printed in the United States of America
16 17 18 19 20 21 Versa 10 9 8 7 6 5 4 3 2 1

Contents

Foreword

It's amazing what filmmakers can accomplish with a green screen. I love to watch documentaries about the making of sci-fi and action films as they show the actors in a studio going through their movements in front of a huge green screen. In that monochromatic environment, their movements seem lifeless and purposeless. Then, however, when they add the virtual background—*voila!*—the actors are now moving about in an alternate reality, and all their movements are magnified and purposeful. The background creates a context, a horizon, that enables a whole new reality to burst into existence.

The beauty of Catholicism is its ability to provide believers with a context—a background—that enables the reality of the kingdom of God to burst into existence in everyday life. Catholicism is a unique way of perceiving all reality: ourselves, others, the world, and God. This Catholic vision, when put into practice, enables Catholics to recognize a cosmos that is filled with goodness and possibility, despite the evils that also lurk. The Catholic vision is one of imagination, joy, selfless love, mercy, and justice, and best of all, the nearness of God. This vision, when lived fully and faithfully, has inspired countless millions to approach the Catholic Church saying, "I want to see as you see."

Mike Leach does an incredible job of articulating this unique, rich, and complex Catholic vision in this book, *Positively Catholic*, which I invite you to read and savor for yourself. Leach says that the Catholic vision can be described as "ideas that point to spiritual realities." Catholicism is a sacramental faith, which means that we rely on signs, symbols, and rituals to make tangible and visible that which is intangible and invisible. Catholicism stimulates the imagination, enabling us to envision an alternate reality—God's kingdom—alongside and within the reality our eyes see. Imagination is not a flight of fancy that puts us out of touch with reality; rather, it gives us the ability to see the world *as it is* while also seeing and recognizing another reality beyond it, visible only with the eyes of faith.

In these brief but delicious twenty-five chapters, Mike Leach helps us view our lives with the Catholic imagination. In this alternate but very real (not virtual!) reality, God lurks in every scene—the divine presence is nearby, not in a distant galaxy. Against the "green screen" of this reality, we see that we have been given a role in the drama of salvation history—a story in which God is the leading actor. Against this backdrop we also discover that we are not performing in a one-person play but participate as members of a huge and mysterious ensemble. The Catholic reality is filled with rich imagery—signs, symbols, and rituals—that add layers of texture to daily yet miraculous life. Finally, this reality is filled with hope, for it tells a story of unparalleled love—and no one can resist a good love story.

Mike Leach does in *Positively Catholic* what Pope Francis urges all of us Catholics to do: move beyond an approach to church that is defined by rules and judgment, and to proclaim the gospel primarily as a way of seeing our lives against the background of a loving and merciful God who is near to us and eager to walk with us.

Joe Paprocki, DMin

Author of *A Church on the Move:*
52 Ways to Get Mission and Mercy in Motion

Preface

A good tree brings you good fruit.
—LUKE 6:43

This is a book of good ideas that bear healthy fruit in our lives: love, joy, peace, patience, kindness, goodness, gratitude, gentleness, faithfulness, and harmony (Galatians 5:22–23).

The ideas come from what Catholics call the "deposit of faith"—a phrase that points to ideas deposited by men and women in Catholic consciousness for the past 2,000 years. Strictly speaking, the deposit of faith refers to a number of Scriptures and traditions as interpreted by bishops and popes but, spiritually seen, it is an open vault so large and deep that no one can withdraw all of its riches in a thousand lifetimes. The deposit of faith is not a limited checking account; it's a trust fund that increases and multiplies. We can deposit into it, and we can withdraw from it, forever and every moment.

The gold standard of the treasury is measured by ideas that bring forth fruits of the Spirit. This book draws on twenty-five of them. They are rich with the positive *stuff* of Catholicism, "the substance of things hoped for, the evidence of things not seen" (Hebrews 11:1). These riches are what the poet Gerard Manley Hopkins called "the dearest freshness deep down things." They are ideas that last, because they are spiritual.

Some of these ideas are universal and common to other faiths, but Catholicism, like Methodism or Judaism or Buddhism, has its own unique take on things, and Catholics experience them in their own familial ways. The chapters first appeared in 2011 as the first part of my book *Why Stay Catholic? Unexpected Answers to a Life-Changing Question*, published by Loyola Press. Some of the ideas presented there had been minimized by the teaching church for a long time, and many readers responded with surprise as if discovering fresh food in the back of their own pantry. Three years later, in 2013, Jorge Mario Bergoglio of Argentina became Pope Francis and the exemplar of many Catholic ideas that had been neglected or ignored, and through his words and deeds they now became as obtainable and nourishing as low-hanging fruit. The folks at Loyola Press thought it would be helpful to have a smaller book than *Why Stay Catholic?*—this book—that spotlighted the Francis effect for readers interested in the core of the nest egg, the heart of the matter, presented in a way that would energize discussion groups as well as individuals.

So, please, continue reading, and for just a while put aside the negative portrait of the church you may have grown up with, or the dark side you sometimes see on television. That picture is incomplete, like a *Mona Lisa* without a smile or a *Pieta* without the embrace. The purpose of this book is to show you the glow of Catholicism, the smile that comes from deep in your heart, and to remind you of its embrace, the kind of embrace Pope Francis gave a severely disfigured man as he kissed the tumors on his cheek. We are all in need of a smile, a hug, a kiss of peace, healing, love, forgiveness, mercy, and joy.

I hope *Positively Catholic* will be a book you can turn to for reminders of the grace that is always with you when life gets you down and your faith seems dim. I've updated some of the examples. I'm grateful to Andrew Yankech at Loyola Press for putting together the study questions at the end of the book so that it can prompt reflection or help folks in a classroom or parish get together and love the faith, live the faith, and share their faith.

Michael Leach

June 2016

The Sacramental Imagination

Though I was blind, now I see.
—JOHN 9:25

Being a Catholic is about seeing the chosen part of things.

+ An infant whose Father's house has many mansions but who chooses to be born in a manger.
+ A man nailed to a cross who is not a victim but unbounded love.
+ A virgin womb. A faithful groom. An empty tomb.
+ A treasure hidden in a field. A coin found. A mustard seed.
+ Eternity in a grain of sand.

Catholicism is about seeing what the eyes cannot see and understanding what is at the heart of things: truth, love, mercy, goodness, beauty, harmony, humility, compassion, gratitude, joy, peace, salvation. It's about seeing the ordinary and perceiving the extraordinary at the same time: the midnight glow of Easter candles that are, in truth, a thousand points of light; the stories of saints, the saga of sinners, and the rumors of angels that inspire and heal us. "It is only with the heart that one sees rightly," wrote Antoine de Saint-Exupery. "What is essential is invisible to the eye."

We don't choose to see the chosen parts of things. It chooses us. It's like when we gaze at the silhouette of a vase. Sometimes we see the vase; then instantly we see two faces. Which is real; which is true? We can't force ourselves to see either one. Both are there. What we see in the moment chooses us.

We see water running down an infant's head at baptism, and suddenly we behold new life. We watch a priest or a sister or a layperson handing out wafers but are aware that God's spiritual child is sharing God's spiritual life with God's spiritual children—and we know that all are somehow mysteriously one. We look at a holy card, a piece of paper, and perceive fidelity, courage, and love. What first appears ordinary catches fire. The mundane turns to gold. A divine alchemy takes place. We see the chosen parts: beauty, love, harmony, joy. This is what is called the "sacramental imagination."

A sacrament points to and opens what is invisible but real. It is an outward sign, instituted by Christ, to give grace. Catholics cherish the seven sacraments of the Church: baptism, confirmation, Holy Communion, reconciliation, marriage, holy orders, and the anointing of the sick. These are the Sacraments with a big *S*. There are also sacraments with a small *s*. We receive the Sacraments once or many times over a lifetime. But we give sacraments every moment of our lives.

✛ We give a sacrament of baptism every time we behold another as a child of God.

✛ We offer a sacrament of reconciliation every time we say to someone "I'm sorry" or "I forgive you."

✛ Every time a wife says to her husband or a husband to his wife, "I love you"—or better, when a husband gets a cold cloth and puts it on his wife's forehead when she has a headache, or when a wife gives her husband a hug for no other reason than she knows he needs it—is a sacrament of marriage.

✛ A sacrament of eucharist happens every time family or friends gather around a table to share in the good of God.

✛ Every time someone decides to live a better life is a sacrament of confirmation.

✛ Everyone who makes a radical commitment to be here not for himself but for God expresses a sacrament of holy orders.

✛ Every time we visit a sick person in a hospital or nursing home and just kiss them on the cheek is an anointing of the sick.

What could be more beautiful?

An old song says, "Little things mean a lot." Sacraments with a small *s* mean everything to those who give them and to those who receive them.

Catholicism is about cultivating our sacramental imagination so that we can see and be the chosen part of things.

"Catholicism is above all a way of seeing," writes theologian Robert Barron in his book *And Now I See*. "Origen of Alexandria once remarked that holiness is seeing with the eyes of Christ. Teilhard de Chardin said, with great passion, that his mission as a Christian thinker was to help people see, and Thomas Aquinas said that the ultimate goal of the Christian life is a 'beatific vision,' an act of seeing."

When I was in seminary studying to be a priest, our English teacher, Fr. Ignatius Burrill, introduced us to the poetry of Gerard Manley Hopkins. He opened my eyes to a sacramental world of beauty beyond words. I'll always remember this verse:

Christ plays in ten thousand places,
Lovely in limbs, and lovely in eyes not his
To the Father through the features of men's faces.

When I was at home that summer, I saw Christ on Clark Street. I was walking toward our apartment near Wrigley Field and passed a down-and-out guy drinking from a bottle in a paper bag. I didn't look him in the eyes. Then I recalled my friend Larry McCauley telling me about a church not far from both of us with a crucified Jesus etched in stone on the wall. A legend under the cross read, "Is it nothing to you who pass by?" Suddenly the man on the street and the man on the cross were one.

Later I saw a little girl playing jacks on the sidewalk in front of her house. She playfully tossed the jacks on the pavement just as God must have flung the stars across the sky. She bounced the little red ball, and it paused in the air as if it were the sun. I thought I was seeing the whole story of creation in a game of jacks.

I looked at many people on my way home that day but saw them differently than I ever had before. Each of them wore a human face, etched in stone or as sunny as July, and each revealed a unique face of Christ. Hopkins's words appeared and disappeared. I saw a person, and I saw who was really there.

As soon as the moment came, just as soon did it go. But I remember it still.

There comes a moment, once—and God help those
Who pass that moment by!—when Beauty stands
looking into the soul with grave, sweet eyes
That sicken at pretty words.

—Cyrano de Bergerac

Fr. Burrill and Larry McCauley taught me that poetry is the best theology. The sacramental imagination, a unique Catholic idea, opens our inner eye to the chosen part of things. St. Bonaventure, a father of the church, counseled his students to "see with the eyes of the soul." The mystic Meister Eckhart said that "we see God with the same eyes that God sees us." Everything is somehow one. "If you have an eye for it," St. Augustine wrote, "the world itself is a sacrament."

"The sacramental imagination" is a phrase popularized by Fr. Andrew Greeley. He adapted it from the theology of his friend Fr. David Tracy, a theologian at the

Divinity School of the University of Chicago, who wrote a seminal book called *The Analogical Imagination*. Fr. Greeley writes in his book, *The Catholic Imagination*:

> Catholics live in an enchanted world, a world of statues and holy water, stained glass and votive candles, saints and religious medals, rosary beads and holy pictures. But these Catholic paraphernalia are mere hints of a deeper and more pervasive religious sensibility which inclines Catholics to see the Holy lurking in creation. As Catholics, we find our houses and our world haunted by a sense that the objects, events and persons of daily life are revelations of grace. (p. 1)

Catholicism, seen through the eye of a needle, is a religion of rules and regulations. Seen with the sacramental imagination, it is a unique take on life, a holy vision, a way of seeing the chosen part of things.

When asked who he was and what he did, Jesus told his disciples, "Come and *see!*" Who can resist an invitation like that?

2

God Is Everywhere

Q. Where is God?
A. Everywhere!
—THE BALTIMORE CATECHISM

A tattered copy of this standard text sat on the desk of every girl and boy in Catholic schools from 1885 till the late 1960s. You will not find a Catholic adult who cannot repeat that remarkable Q and A. It's a simple expression of faith that points to the chosen part of *everything*.

I was surprised not to find anything like it in the new *Catechism of the Catholic Church*, but that may just be me. *The Baltimore Catechism* was a sixty-two-page booklet, and the Vatican catechism has 928 pages and weighs more than my brain. I did find the word *omnipotence* five times in the index but no mention of the word *omnipresence*. I thought, *Gee, this is like having a classic songbook of the Beatles that doesn't include "Here, There, and Everywhere."* On the other hand, *The Baltimore Catechism* doesn't tell us what Easter is about. It's helpful to have more than one catechism in the house.

7

That's because we can never hear enough of this wonderful Catholic idea: God is everywhere. We know from the movie, *The Big Lebowski,* that the Dude abides but we know from Scripture and tradition that Grace abounds. Grace runs through everything because God is "here, there, and everywhere." What could be more comforting?

> *Wither shall I go from thy spirit? Or wither shall I flee from thy presence? If I ascend up into heaven, thou art there: if I make my bed in hell, behold thou art there. If I take the wings of the morning, and dwell in the uttermost parts of the sea, even there shall thy hand lead me and thy right hand shall hold me.*
> —PSALM 139:7–10, KJV

> *Yea, though I walk through the valley of the shadow of death, I will fear no evil: for thou art with me; thy rod and thy staff they comfort me.*
> —PSALM 23:4, KJV

At the end of the novel *Diary of a Country Priest* a young priest lies dying, waiting for an old pastor to arrive and administer last rites. The friend at his bedside worries that the pastor won't get there on time and the priest will not receive the church's last blessing. The dying priest senses his concern and, in a halting but clear voice, says, "Does it matter? Grace is everywhere."

The church may not always be there for us, but Catholicism teaches that God is everywhere for us. That's all that matters.

Jesus taught us to look for God in the birds of the air and the lilies of the field. When I was a young priest (I left after three years to marry), I once said a Mass for children who were sitting in a field of dandelions next to a lake with frogs popping out like Muppets. I read the gospel on the lilies of the field and then asked the children: "Each one of you, go and choose a flower and just look at it." They scattered and each found a pet dandelion and put their face close to it. "Just look at it," I said. "And see how it grows." The children smiled as the yellow lions smiled back. I waited. I whispered, "If I could look into your eyes right now, I would see a flower. God is everywhere, and each of you is baptizing a flower!"

> The fullness of joy is to behold God in everything.
> —St. Julian of Norwich

Shortest sermon I ever gave.

Finding God in all things is the foundation of Ignatian spirituality. But to say that God is in all things is not to say that everything is God. That would be pantheism, literally "All *is* God." God and creation are not the same. God is greater than the sum of all the parts of all that he has made. "God is All in all" (1 Corinthians 15:28), "God is love" (1 John 4:8), and,

> The day of my spiritual wakening was the day I saw—and knew I saw—all things in God and God in all things.
> —Mechtild of Magdeburg

incredibly, "We live and move and have our being in God" (Acts 17:28). These words spark our sacramental imagination and help us understand an awesome truth. We are like fish that swim in an ocean of love: the fish are in the ocean, and the ocean is in the fish. We are in God and God is in us. We are swimming in God but don't even know it. The key to peace—and to swimming effortlessly through life—is to come to know who and where we really are. God is love, God is everywhere, and everywhere is in God. Wherever we are, God is always present! We don't have to look far to find God. He is within us and all around us because we are within him. This idea has tremendous practical applications for prayer and daily living.

Here is what religious educator Michael Morwood has to say about the God who is so everywhere that "the heavens and the heavens above the heavens cannot contain him" (Psalm 68:33):

> It makes a big difference how we pray if we view God as a person in heaven or, as the *Baltimore Catechism* put it, if we view God "everywhere." For many of us prayer has been an effort to contact an "elsewhere God." What happens when we shift our attention to an "everywhere God"—a sustaining Presence in all, through all, never absent, never distant, not in one place more than in any other place, a Presence "in whom we live and move and have our being"?
>
> There is a new story emerging in consciousness, one that evokes awe, wonder, and reverence as it expands our notion of God. We are beginning to understand that God is not limited to a place and only vaguely present in the universe. We are beginning to appreciate a God alive in every particle in the billions of galaxies beyond us and in the grass or pavement beneath our feet. God is here, everywhere, and always with us.

May we open our minds and hearts
to the presence of God in us.
May God-in-us,
the "everywhere God,"
find generous and courageous expression
in our words and actions
as we undertake
to make the reign of God
evident in our world.
Amen.
(Michael Morwood, from *Praying a New Story*,
pp. 7, 138)

God is present in the furthest star and in the smallest seed. God is present before and after we are born and in every detail of our lives. God is love and wisdom and available to us in each and every moment because we are, literally, in love. It only takes eyes to see.

Did you ever see that wonderful black-and-white movie from the 1950s, *The Incredible Shrinking Man?* The hero, Scott Carey, blond, blue-eyed, and tall, is sailing his boat in the ocean beneath an infinite sky. Suddenly a mist appears and covers him with a radioactive dust. Slowly he goes from six feet to three feet to three inches to infinitesimal. At the end of the movie this dot of a man is walking in his garden through blades of grass that are taller than trees, amongst towering flowers that look like planets and suns, and sailing on a twig over a puddle as large as a lake. Suddenly, Scott *sees*. He is still at home in the universe! It has shrunk but God is everywhere. We hear his inner voice:

> So close—the infinitesimal and the infinite. But suddenly, I knew they were really the two ends of the same concept. The unbelievably small and the unbelievably vast eventually meet—like the closing of a gigantic circle. I looked up, as if somehow I would grasp the heavens. The universe, worlds beyond number, God's silver tapestry spread across the night. And in that moment, I knew the answer to the riddle of the infinite. I had thought in terms of man's own limited dimension. I had presumed upon nature. That existence begins and ends in man's conception, not nature's. And I felt my body dwindling, melting, becoming nothing. My fears melted away. And in their place came acceptance. All this vast majesty of creation, it had to mean something. And then I meant something, too! Yes, smaller than the smallest, I meant something, too. To God, there is no zero. I still exist!

The Catholic idea that God is everywhere is a source of infinite joy. God is love, and that's where we live. Love does not look down and judge. Love teaches us how to live among flowers and to swim in an ocean of love.

3

God Finds Us When
We Least Expect Him

*Christmas, Good Friday, Easter—their message is
not that we must appease an angry God but that
a God of love has found us!*
—THOMAS O'MEARA, OP, ATTRIBUTED

Isn't that wonderful! We don't have to look for God. God
is not only everywhere, but God is always finding us!

God finds us when we least expect him. He finds us
when we are lost in sin, and he finds us, too, when we're
lost in the sacrament of the present moment. This is a
beautiful idea expressed in Catholic poems and stories
throughout the ages. The deposit of faith is filled to overflowing with tales of God's love.

The poet Francis Thompson (1859–1907) writes beau-
tifully about our flight from God and God's pursuit of us
in *The Hound of Heaven*:

I fled Him, down the nights and down the days;
I fled Him, down the arches of the years;
I fled Him, down the labyrinthine ways
    Of my own mind; and in the mist of tears
I hid from Him, and under running laughter.
        Up vistaed hopes I sped;
        And shot, precipitated,
Adown Titanic glooms of chasmèd fears,
From those strong Feet that followed, followed after.
        But with unhurrying chase,
        And unperturbèd pace,
    Deliberate speed, majestic instancy,
        They beat—and a Voice beat
        More instant than the Feet—
    "All things betray thee, who betrayest Me."

And finally, when we are out of breath and can run no more, we hear God's call:

    "Rise, clasp My hand, and come!"

. . .

    "Ah, fondest, blindest, weakest,
    I am He Whom thou seekest!
Thou dravest love from thee, who dravest Me!"

We can no more escape God than a wave can escape the ocean. The wave is in the ocean, and the ocean is in the wave. God is with us whether we want him to be or not. St. Augustine wrote, "Our hearts are restless until they rest in Thee." We will know salvation, sooner or later. Sooner is better.

The parable of the lost son (Luke 15:11–32) gives us assurance. A restless young man asks his affluent father for his share of the inheritance. The generous father gives it to him. The son goes off and squanders it, living a life of debauchery, sleeping with pigs and eating their swill. The prodigal son, like the lost soul in *The Hound of Heaven*, cries out, "I have recklessly forgotten Your glory, O Father!" He begins crawling back home, praying that his father will receive him as a penitent and let him back in the house, if only as a hired hand.

And here is the best part, the part that warms and enfolds us like a favorite quilt. Here is a reason that I am still Catholic:

> While he was still far off, his father saw him and was filled with compassion; he ran and put his arms around him and kissed him. Then the son said to him, "Father, I have sinned against heaven and before you; I am no longer worthy to be called your son." But the father said to his slaves, "Quickly, bring out a robe—the best one—and put it on him; put a ring on his finger and sandals on his feet. And get the fatted calf and kill it, and let us eat and celebrate; for this son of mine was dead and is alive again; he was lost and is found!" And they began to celebrate. (Luke 15:20–24, NRSV)

The father makes the first move! The father races to embrace the son before the son can say a word!

God finds us, again and again, when we least expect him. He finds us because he never left us, giving us everything always, and giving us even more when we recognize who we are and where Love is. Jesus assures us that God can never leave us: "I will not leave you orphaned. . . . I am in my Father, and you in me, and I in you." (John 14:18, 20). Repentance happens when we realize that we are in Jesus and that Jesus and the Father are *one* (John 10:30).

> God never tires of forgiving us; we are the ones who tire of seeking his mercy.
> —POPE FRANCIS

> God's love for us is freely given and unearned, surpassing all we could ever hope for or imagine. He does not love us because we have merited it or are worthy of it. God loves us, rather, because he is true to his own nature.
> —POPE JOHN PAUL II

God is the Hound of Heaven. He finds us in our despair. It makes no difference what we have done—God is already there. This is an idea from the deposit of faith that makes it easy for me to stay Catholic.

God not only finds us when we are lost; he also finds us when we aren't even looking for him. He finds us in the present moment. Long before Eckhart Tolle wrote *The Power of Now*, Jean-Pierre de Caussade, SJ (1675–1751) wrote *The Sacrament of the Present Moment*, and Brother Lawrence of the Resurrection's (c. 1611–1691) teachings were compiled in *Practice of the Presence of God*. In the first chapter of this book we learned about the seven sacraments with a small *s*. The *eighth* sacrament—the sacrament of the present moment—opens our eyes to a God of surprises who comes to us when we least expect him.

When Thomas Merton was a young monk at the Abbey of Gethsemane, he sometimes had to go to Louisville for a doctor's appointment. At first the hurrying crowds distracted him from his endeavor to pray always. But one day Merton just let go. He stood still and looked. Suddenly the whole city seemed to glow with the grace of God. "How do you tell people," he asked himself, "that they are walking around shining like the sun!"

That is a sacrament of the present moment.

In the movie *Field of Dreams* Shoeless Joe Jackson asks the hero, Ray Kinsella, "Is this heaven?"

"No," he says. "It's Iowa."

Heaven begins on the spot where we are standing. Funny thing, but like Ray, I think I first had a sense of God's presence playing baseball. Let me tell you about it.

I was eight or nine years old. Maybe ten. It doesn't matter, because when it happened, time stood still, and I was eternal.

In my big-city neighborhood the kids played softball on cross streets where manhole covers served as bases. The fourteen-incher would pop its stitches, but you used it until it was a pillow. Even so, you'd better not smack it too far down the middle, or it might crack the window of an apartment building. You had to pull the ball to the street on the left or punch it down the street to the right. You began playing after school and didn't stop until your mother called your name from a wooden porch or the sun sank behind the skyline.

Little guys like me sat on the curb until one of the big guys put us in, usually on the street to the right. I'd often drop the ball, especially hard line drives, and rarely hit one past the pitcher. I wanted to play well and not goof up, and I thought about what the other kids were thinking of me. Then one evening (or more accurately this one sacramental moment) while the sun was painting the apartment windows gold, I stopped wanting, stopped thinking.

And heaven said hello.

I was in right field. The ball popped off the bat like grease from a frying pan and lofted high over my head. All I did was *see* it and turn and follow its path. I wasn't thinking about it. Just running, aware of each step, each move of my arms, as if in slow motion, knowing exactly where the ball would come down. At just the right moment, without looking, my fingers reached out and the softball fell onto my hands like a dove. I ran a few more steps, turned, held it up, and smiled!

The big guys cheered. Then the moment vanished.

But to this day, sixty years later, I can remember that golden instant when time stood still and I felt one with the ball, the sun, the street, and yes, let's say it, love.

God is love, an unbelievable oneness that comes to awareness when you least expect it: in the sacrament of the present moment. Baseball first taught me not to worry about the past or plan for the future but simply to pay attention to the ball. I'd need many reminders throughout my life, but I began to learn: God envelops us when we least expect it.

I don't remember what happened after that catch, but I remember other moments of oneness that came suddenly but never lasted more than an inning. Just as quickly as one came, I would take pride in it or dwell on it or try to do it again, and it was gone.

God finds us when we forget about ourselves and live in the present. Awareness catches *us*, but the moment falls apart when we try to pin it against the wall of our mind like a butterfly. It comes to us on colorful see-through wings. And as soon as we take credit for it, it vanishes.

But we never forget it.

Its promise keeps us going—and finds us again when we least expect it.

Everyone of every religion and of no religion has these wonderful moments. I grew up with them in a world of Catholic poems and stories and friends. Still Catholic? Why not?

4

Nothing Can Separate Us from the Love of God—*Nothing!*

Neither death, nor life, nor angels, nor rulers, nor things
present, nor things to come, nor powers, nor height, nor
depth, nor anything else in all creation, will be able to
separate us from the love of God in Christ Jesus our Lord!
—ROMANS 8:38–39, NRSV

What could be more beautiful? No matter what we do or how bad we think we are, nothing can separate us from the love of God. How could it? "We live and move and have our being in God" (Acts 17:28). Can anyone separate a wave from the ocean or a sunbeam from the sun? Catholicism teaches that we are literally in Jesus, and Jesus, who is one with the Father, is in us (John 14:18, 20). "We are syllables," wrote Caryll Houselander, "of the perfect Word!" "God hugs us," said Hildegarde of Bingen. "We are encircled by the arms of the mystery of God."

When Jesus saved the adulteress about to be stoned, he didn't say, "Sin no more and I will not condemn you." He said, "I do not condemn you. *Now* go and sin no more." We first experience God's embrace, and *then* our life changes forever. It all begins with a spiritual idea. Can there be a more joy-making idea than this one?

I saw a beautiful demonstration of this idea at a Catholic convention many years ago. Late at night I took the hotel elevator to a floor where the host organization had a hospitality suite for the conference speakers, a who's who of Catholicism. People packed the room in clusters, ice crackling in cocktail glasses, smoke swirling from cigarettes. My eyes immediately went to the far corner of the room where a nun sat on a sofa, a thin young man resting his head on her chest. The Sister was Jeannine Gramick, a friend whose book on ministering to gays and lesbians in the church I had just published. The boy was so thin, and he seemed so sad. I wondered: does he have AIDS? Jeannine touched his hair with her fingers, gently, like the feathers of an angel. I thought for a moment that someone had moved the *Pieta* from St. Peter's Basilica to this hotel on the outskirts of Chicago. I was aware that the institutional church did not go out of its way to embrace gay Catholics, and I could not take my eyes off this Catholic Sister who was demonstrating—quietly, without fanfare, in the corner of a room—the basic Catholic truth that nothing can separate us from the love of God—*nothing*.

Just as nothing can separate us from the love of God—not death, not sin, not anything—nothing can separate us from one another. We are literally one with one another. When Jesus said, "Love your neighbor as yourself," I think he meant it literally. We *are* our neighbor, and our neighbor is *us*. Jesus said, "I and my Father are one," and then went on to teach us how to pray by saying, "*Our* Father . . ." We are all, each of us, brothers and sisters, children of God, made in the image and likeness of love. What could be more beautiful?

Vickie and I used to go to the Saturday evening Mass at a small working-class parish miles from our home. The church had as many people kneeling in the pews as Wrigley Field has fans sitting in the bleachers during a thunderstorm. But the few people who did attend went there for one reason. The priest gave the same sermon, in different words, every single Saturday of the year. He preached the everlasting love of God in Jesus Christ. His words weren't fancy, but they were authentic. He meant what he said. The parishioners could not get enough.

Did you know that the passage that leads off this chapter appears many times in the Catholic lectionary? We cannot hear it enough.

This passage is the second reading on the eighteenth Sunday in Ordinary Time, Year A. You will also hear it on the weekday of the thirtieth week in Ordinary Time. It also appears in the Proper of Saints, numbers 538, 592, and 642a. Not to mention in Commons, number 716. Did I forget to mention that it also appears in Ritual Masses,

> *The love of Christ is more powerful than sin and death. St. Paul explains that Christ came to forgive sin, and that his love is greater than any sin, stronger than all my personal sins or those of anyone else. This is the faith of the Church. This is the Good News of God's love that the Church proclaims throughout history, and that I proclaim to you today: God loves you with an everlasting love. He loves you in Christ Jesus, his Son.*
> —POPE JOHN PAUL II

numbers 792 and 802, in Masses for Various Needs, numbers 863 and 869, and in Masses for the Dead, number 1014?

When is the last time you heard or, if you are a priest, gave a sermon on, "Nothing can separate us from the love of God?" It's one of the most neglected ideas in our spiritual deposit of faith.

And it's one of the best reasons I can think of for anyone to say, "I am still Catholic."

5

God's Will for Us Is More Wonderful Than Anything We Can Imagine

Q: Why did God make you?
A: He made me to know him, to love him, and to serve him
in this world, and to be happy with him forever in heaven.
—*THE BALTIMORE CATECHISM*

God, infinitely perfect and blessed in himself, in a plan of
sheer goodness freely created man to make him share in his
own blessed life. For this reason, at every time and in every
place, God draws close to man. He calls man to seek him,
to know him, to love him with all his strength.
—*THE CATECHISM OF THE CATHOLIC CHURCH* (FIRST THREE SENTENCES)

Dr. Thomas Hora (1914–1995) was a pathbreaking psychiatrist who taught that problems are psychological and that solutions are spiritual. His core principle was the Genesis revelation that man is "made in the image and likeness of God." He called his approach to health and healing Existential Metapsychiatry. Much of it is based on the words of Jesus. I was a student of Dr. Hora at the New York Institute of Metapsychiatry for three years. He wasn't religious, but his insights not only enriched my life but also shed light on much of "the good stuff" in my religion that has been forgotten, neglected, or ignored for too long. As my friend theologian Jack Shea once remarked, "We Catholics take help from wherever we can find it!" Dr. Hora once said that there are three kinds of people:

✛ those who are here for themselves
✛ those who are here for others
✛ those who are here for God

The first "mode of being in the world" is self-confirmatory and leads to self-destruction. The second is the flip side of the first; when we do good to feel good we also get in trouble. The third—to be here for God—is the key to eternal life. How similar to the teachings quoted from the two Catholic catechisms above!

When we are here for God—when we endeavor to know, love, and serve him in this world—we not only share in God's own blessed life but also begin to realize happiness with him forever. Eternity begins on the spot where we are standing.

The Catechism of the Catholic Church opens with this epigraph: "This is eternal life, that they may know you, the only true God, and Jesus Christ, whom you have sent" (John 17:3). That same epigraph is on the very first page of Dr. Hora's book *Dialogues in Metapsychiatry*, and underneath it: "The meaning and purpose of life is to come to know Reality."

When we come to know God who is Love and in whose image we are made, and Jesus Christ whom Love has sent as a light into the world (John 8:12), we cannot help but choose to be here for God, and to love and serve him because we see that God's will for us is more wonderful than anything we can imagine.

God doesn't want to hurt us. His will for us is good, pleasing and perfect (Romans 12:2). We hurt when we forget or ignore Reality: what and where we really are—likenesses of Love who live and move and have our being in Love. The key is to know it and to show it. The church teaches that we suffer when we disobey the will of God. Dr. Hora put it this way: "We suffer from what we want and what we don't want." When we don't want what Love wants, trouble is sure to follow. Isn't it helpful to read about the same truths in different words?

What does God want? God wants us to know we're in Love. Jesus asks us to be that love in the world. "Love one

> *God is love. On this solid rock the entire faith of the Church is based.*
> —POPE BENEDICT XVI

another as I have loved you" (John 15:12). That's all we need to study, that's all we need to know. It's the beginning of eternal life. "God is love. Whoever lives in love lives in God, and God in him" (1 John 4:16, NIV).

So why do bad things happen to good people? What's up with that?

I don't know. And neither does anybody else.

You won't find me saying Catholicism has the final word on that question. Indeed, to its credit, the church has always said it is a mystery. Like you and everyone else I've been wrestling with that question my whole life. I've talked with friends about it over kitchen tables. I've read the works of Catholic saints and Zen sages and Indian seers. Like anybody else, when it comes to pain, loss, and depression, I look for help wherever I can find it. As a publisher I've asked many Catholic authors whose insights I appreciate to write books on suffering just so I could read what they discovered and pass it along to others. When it comes to the question, why do bad things happen to good people, Dr. Hora gave me a good lead. Any question beginning with "Why?" he said, is futile. When you start asking why, you become like a snake chasing its own tail. You get dizzy with follow-up questions that go nowhere, like "Who's to blame? How do I feel? What's wrong? What should I do? How should I do it? What shouldn't I do? Why shouldn't I do it? Why am I going nuts?!" That's not spiritual inquiry; that's cable news talk. The question, "Why did God make you?" is really "What is your purpose in life?" Questions beginning with "What?" are helpful. "If we know what," Dr. Hora wrote, "then we know how."

So then, what is the meaning of suffering? What's it all about, Alfie? The 928-page *Catechism* has only one listing for "Suffering" in its 107-page index, and that refers to a brief paragraph on the

> *Not everything is immediately good to those who seek God, but everything is capable of becoming good.*
> —TEILHARD DE CHARDIN,
> *THE DIVINE MILIEU*

suffering of Christ. What can we learn from the spiritual deposit of faith?

Mother Teresa tells the story of consoling a little girl who was sick and in pain. She told the child, "You should be happy that God sends you suffering because your sufferings are proof that God loves you very much. Your sufferings are kisses from Jesus."

"Then, Mother," said the girl, "please ask Jesus not to kiss me so much."

Mother Teresa got the joke on herself. Suffering is not a good. When we tell someone that we're hurting and they, in sincerity, say to us, "Don't worry. God never sends us more than we can handle," be polite, but remember the Mother Teresa story. The philosopher Ludwig Wittgenstein observed, "What can be said at all can be said clearly, and whereof what one cannot speak, thereon one must be silent." Fr. Matt Hoffman, my freshman English teacher in high school, a teddy bear of a man, told us the best response to someone at a funeral parlor or in a hospital is a hug. A real one.

"God had one son on earth without sin," wrote Augustine, "but never one without suffering." Dr. Hora used to say that "suffering isn't necessary, but it is inevitable." I say, nobody gets out of this thing alive. Robert Ellsberg writes in *The Saints' Guide to Happiness*:

> The saints do not teach us how to avoid suffering; they teach us how to suffer. They do not provide the "meaning" of suffering. But they lived by the assurance

that there is a meaning or truth *at the heart of life* that suffering is powerless to destroy. They did not believe that suffering is good but that God is good and that "neither death nor life, nor height nor depth" can deprive us of access to that good if we truly desire it. They found that there is no place that is literally "god-forsaken," but that in every situation, even the most grim and painful, there is a door that leads to love, to fullness of life, to happiness. This is the deepest mystery of the gospel. Our task, if we would learn from the saints, is to find that door and enter in.

Of all the authors I've asked to write a book about suffering, the one who moved me the most is Fr. William O'Malley, SJ, in *Redemptive Suffering*. A high school teacher of religion and English for almost fifty years, Bill knows how to talk to kids. And that's the kind of language I need when shivering in awe at the magnitude of the mystery of evil. Like the priest I wrote about in chapter 4, whose every sermon was on the love of Jesus, Bill draws readers to Jesus on the cross as our exemplar. He tells a story that stuns us with its simplicity:

> One time during Easter week, a frighteningly intelligent little boy named Cisco, who had gone to all the Holy Week ceremonies, asked me, "Father, if God really loved his Son so much, why would he ask him to go through such an awful, awful death?" My only answer to him then is my only answer to him now: To show us how it's done. With dignity.

Bill O'Malley lives what he teaches. He's one of those guys whose face is a road map of suffering and joy. He can wince and smile at the

> *The Son of God suffered unto the death, not that men might not suffer, but that their sufferings might be like his.*
> —GEORGE MACDONALD

same time. If you saw the movie *The Exorcist*, Bill was the kindly priest at the end of the movie whom Linda Blair, no longer possessed, runs up to and hugs. That's the kind of guy he is.

The mystery of a God who is all good and a world riddled with good and evil is just that: a riddle. Andrew Greeley writes eloquently about a God who suffers with us. Others speculate that God knows nothing about suffering but is a power we can tap into to help carry our cross. Richard Rohr sheds practical light in *Job and the Mystery of Suffering*:

> The human question when we are hanging on our cross is first, "Why is my life like this?" (We all probably start there.) But grace leads us to an amazing and startling recognition, "My life is not about me." Think about that for the rest of your years. My life is not about me—this is the great and saving revelation that comes only from the whirlwind, and we are never ready for it.
>
> It helps to remember that our suffering is not just for ourselves and not just about ourselves. Joyfully borne, suffering also helps other people. Redemptive suffering is, I believe, a radical call to a deeper life and deeper

faith that affects not only the self but others. I visit hospitals and see people suffering with resignation and even joy. Afterward, I feel my energy quadrupled. That's no small thing—the life we can share with others when we unite in the spirit of Christ's crucifixion and resurrection.

Every October I travel to St. Mary of the Lake Seminary in Mundelein, Illinois, for a two-day retreat with twenty of my classmates from 1966. Each year four of us volunteer to give a brief presentation to stimulate discussion and prayer. We sit in a circle in a classroom with tall windows letting in light. A few years ago I chose to talk about suffering simply because it's a topic I think about a lot. I don't remember what I said, but I was as sincere as the simple priest who always talks about Jesus. At the end of the presentation Tom Smith said, "Thank you. I have to talk about something." He told us about his beloved daughter who had recently committed suicide. He talked for ten minutes. He was sitting on a wooden desk-chair that was like a cross holding him down, but he gave us his wounded heart, and at just the right moment Johnny Pritcher stood up and said, "All right, guys, group hug!" We all rose and embraced, and tears flowed, and love passed from one guy to another to the whole world.

That was a moment when I understood something about suffering and the overwhelming love of God. I stay Catholic because of the love of God that comes through friends.

6

The Mystics, or There's a Way of Knowing That Has Nothing to Do with the Brain

In the days ahead you will either be a mystic (one who has experienced God for real) or nothing at all.
—KARL RAHNER

There's a big difference between knowing God and knowing *about* God. Words about God are not God. The words we read in this or any other book are not "the truth that sets us free" (John 8:32). The Zen master says, "The finger pointing in the direction of the moon is not the moon." The scientist Alfred Korzybski reminds us, "The map is not the territory." *A Course in Miracles* says, "Words are symbols of symbols and thus twice removed from reality." *The Catechism of the Catholic Church* says, "We do not believe in formulas but in the realities they express." And Jesus says, "God is Spirit, and they that worship him must worship him in spirit and in truth" (John 4:24).

Words change. Maps amend. Formulas revise. And cat-echisms come and go. But the chosen part of things, that which lasts, which is spiritual, remains forever. Catholicism is not knowing about God but coming to know God.

How do we do that?

We can start by paying attention to what spiritual masters have to say. Theologian Karl Rahner, SJ (1904–1984), widely acknowledged as "the Thomas Aquinas of the twen-tieth century," wrote in *Encounters with Silence*:

> Thanks to your mercy, O Infinite God, I know some-thing about you not only through concepts and words, but through experience. I have actually *known you* through living contact. I have *met you* in joy and suf-fering. For you are the first and last experience of my life. Yes, really you yourself, not just a concept of you, not just the name which we ourselves have given to you! You have descended upon me in water and the Spirit, in my baptism. And then there was no question of my convincing or excogitating anything about you. Then my reason with its extravagant cleverness was still silent. Then, without asking me, you made yourself my poor heart's destiny.

That's awesome. There's a way of knowing God that has nothing to do with formulas, concepts, or even words. Ironically, the title for this chapter was inspired by my favorite atheist, Woody Allen. In his movie *Manhattan*, he says to Diane Keaton, "The brain is the most over-rated organ. There's a way of knowing that has nothing to do with the brain." The Zen masters speak about direct knowing. The Catholic mystics speak about direct consciousness of the awareness of God. Bernard McGinn in his magisterial three-volume work *The Presence of God: A History of Western Christian Mysticism* writes:

> The ways in which this special form of encounter with God have been understood are multiple. One thing that all Christian mystics have agreed on is that the experience in itself defies conceptualization and verbalization, in part or in whole."

St. Teresa of Ávila (1515–1582), the great mystical doctor of the church, described "a consciousness of the presence of God of such a kind that I could not possibly doubt that God was within me and I was totally engulfed in him." St. Teresa, by the way, was the author of this famous spiritual quote:

> Christ has no body on earth but yours; no hands, no feet on earth but yours. Yours are the eyes with which he looks compassionately on this world. Yours are the feet with which he walks to do good. Yours are the hands with which he blesses all the world. Christ has no body now on earth but yours.

You're familiar with it because you have seen it on T-shirts, tote bags, mugs, and mouse pads. Who says people today aren't interested in being mystics?

The mystical experience is characterized by a sense of oneness. Our eyes are Christ's eyes beholding the world.

It's impossible to define. But imagine a sunbeam being suddenly aware that it is one with the sun and all the other rays of the sun. It knows no separation. Or imagine a wave conscious of its oneness with the ocean and all the other waves. In truth, there is no sun or sunbeam. There is only light. There are no waves. There is only water. That is direct knowing. It is non-knowing.

That's about the best I can do.

So let me tell you a story. Again it involves Dr. Thomas Hora, who was not Catholic but who unlocked the spiritual wisdom in my faith with extraordinary grace.

I was leaving his office on West 72 Street near Central Park on a bright October afternoon. He had said to me, "You are God's special child." Nothing I had not heard many times since first grade at St. Andrew's, but it stuck this time. I remember standing on the corner of Central Park West, waiting for a bus, and suddenly, without my willing it, the words disappeared, and I *knew.* I stood there, not moving, and it was like the world wasn't moving either, but it was, at just the right speed. It was a sunny day, and you could trace the veins on the leaves of trees a block away and feel the warm breeze and hear the silence amidst the buzz of the street. I looked at the people walking on this side and that, strolling in the park with their dogs or sitting on a bench with their books and it was a moment like Thomas Merton must have experienced as he stood on a street corner in Louisville, Kentucky, and thought, *There is no way of telling people that they are all walking around shining like the sun!* It was one of those moments when all the planets and all the buses and all the people and all the squirrels are just where they are supposed to be. It was like that long-ago afternoon when a softball floated like a butterfly into my hands on a side street near Wrigley Field. Like the day I saw Christ on Clark Street, drinking whiskey from a bottle in a paper bag. Is this what St. Teresa was talking about? Is this what mysticism is about?

> *The eye with which I see God is the same eye with which God sees me.*
> —Meister Eckhart

> *Then I saw a new heaven and a new earth; for the first heaven and the first earth had passed away.*
> —Revelation 21:1, NRSV

Seeing the everyday world with eyes not ours?

Have you had an experience like that? I bet you have. It doesn't last long, but you remember it. And its promise keeps you going.

The finger pointing in the direction of the moon is not the moon, but it's helpful to have spiritual directors—people or icons or a Bible or a spiritual book—to point us in the right direction. I have always found spiritual reading the best trigger for letting go and letting God. This practice is part of an ancient Catholic tradition called *lectio divina*, or holy reading. Have you ever been reading a spiritual book and suddenly the mind stands still, the book falls, and you know what the psalmist meant: "Be still, and know that I am God!" (Psalm 46:10, NRSV) Every now and then it helps to be given a finger.

Moments of awareness when we are conscious of the presence of God don't come often to anyone. As we learned in chapter 3, God comes when we least expect him. It's all about God, not us. What we can do is be interested in God and the things of God and . . . maybe . . . sometime . . . without notice . . . *an Easter moment!* I don't know a better way to put it. And it's one big reason, since Catholicism is the *locus* where my interest was first sparked, that I am Catholic still.

7

The Mystical Body of Christ

*No man is an island, entire of itself; every man is a piece
of the continent, a part of the main. . . . Any man's death
diminishes me, because I am involved in mankind.*
—JOHN DONNE, *DEVOTIONS UPON EMERGENT OCCASIONS*

*If one part of the body suffers, every part suffers with it.
If one part is honored, every part rejoices with it.*
—1 CORINTHIANS 12:26

We were eating brunch at our favorite diner. Vickie
asked me what I was going to work on when we got home.
"Chapter 7," I said, "'The Mystical Body.' It's a tough one."

"Can I help you?" she asked.

"Sure," I answered. "What do you think the Mystical
Body of Christ is?"

She picked up a French fry and held it to the side of
her head as if it were a quill and she was poised to write.
"Well," she said, "we're all part of one body, and Christ is
here to help us."

"That's it," I said, "except a lot of people think it refers only to Catholics."

She bit into her French fry. "That can't be."

"Why not?"

"Because Christ died for all of us."

"Thanks," I said. "You just helped me."

Pope Pius XII popularized the phrase Mystical Body of Christ in his 1943 encyclical *Mystici Corporis Christi*. He described the church as a mystical union of all Christians with Jesus as their head. Twenty-two years later the Second Vatican Council gave the world *Lumen Gentium,* or *Light of the World,* a historic document that expanded the term to include, at least potentially, everybody of all time because . . . well . . . Christ died for all of us.

Still, many Catholics to this day think that this beautiful phrase points not to the moon but to a satellite. When Therese Borchard and I wrote our book, *I Like Being Catholic,* we wrote to hundreds of Catholics, famous and ordinary like us. The late, great Cardinal O'Connor of New York wrote back, "The most amazing thing to me about being Catholic is that I am able to unite myself in faith with men and women not only throughout the world but throughout the centuries." John O'Connor didn't think in a box. Like Vickie, he knew: Jesus came for all of us, the living, the dead, and those to come. For God there is no BC and AD. There is only now.

We can, however, trace the literary DNA of this concept to the corpus of letters written by St. Paul in the first century:

Just as the body is one and has many members, and all the members of the body, though many, are one body, so it is with Christ. (1 Corinthians 12:12, NRSV)

We were all baptized by one Spirit into one body—whether Jews or Greeks, slave or free—and we were all given the one Spirit to drink. Now the body is not made up of one part but of many. (1 Corinthians 12:13–14, NIV)

And so it is. We are all baptized—whether by water or desire—into one *Spirit,* given one *Spirit* to drink, are indeed *one spiritual body*! Talk about the chosen part of things! There is nothing in this idea that imprisons us in bodies of flesh that break and get sick and turn to dust. No one can restrict membership to the Mystical Body of Christ as if it were some kind of religious country club. We are *all* members of one spiritual body! Mystical means "of a spiritual nature." It wasn't Oprah who famously said, "We are not human beings having a spiritual experience; we are spiritual beings having a human experience." It was Teilhard de Chardin (*The Phenomenon of Man,* 1955), the Catholic paleontologist who spent his life looking at rocks and seeing eternity. Remember reading in the last chapter that "God is Spirit, and those who worship him must

> *We are already one. But we imagine that we are not. And what we have to recover is our original unity. What we have to be is what we are.*
> —THOMAS MERTON, SPEECH IN CALCUTTA, 1968

worship in spirit and truth" (John 4:24, NRSV)? That's
what it's all about!

When I was studying philosophy in seminary way back
when, Fr. John "Spanky" McFarland, SJ, wrote on the
blackboard: "You are an *unum per se*!" He wrote it so hard
the chalk broke and splintered into pieces, like the beginning of a universe. He wanted us to know: this is important! Spanky was a great teacher but never fully explained
what he meant by *unum per se*. It was one of those truths
he wanted us to *see*.

The philosopher Gottfried Wilhelm Leibniz (1646–
1716) coined those words. His name reminds me of a Mel
Brooks character out of *Young Frankenstein* but in fact,
Leibniz was one of the great minds of the seventeenth century and used the controversial term *unum per se* to describe
the remarkable unity of body, mind, and soul. Three hundred years later we pick up magazines with names like *Body,
Mind, and Spirit* on coffee tables in our doctors' offices.

While Fr. McFarland never fully explained *unum per
se*, our English teacher Fr. Burrill pointed us in the right
direction. He taught us Catholic poetry. He taught us
Gerard Manley Hopkins, who taught us all that each of us

Acts in God's eye what in God's eye he is—
Christ—for Christ plays in ten thousand places,
Lovely in limbs, and lovely in eyes not his
To the Father through the features of men's faces.

Not only is the hand bone connected to the neck bone and the neck bone connected to the brain and the brain to the mind and the mind to the soul—all one—but I am part of you and you are part of me and we are all one in Christ. I wouldn't put it that way to a Jewish or Muslim or Buddhist friend but they, too, *see* the chosen part of things.

The New Physics also points us in the direction of the moon and sheds light on the Mystical Body of Christ. It demonstrates that there is, in fact, no space between any of us. It talks about "the butterfly effect," how when a butterfly flaps its wings in India a storm can brew in Indiana. What happens to each of us happens to all of us. When a child in Calcutta goes hungry, a child in California can sense her pain. When a Samaritan helps a wounded man on the side of the road, a hospital goes up two thousand years later. What blesses one blesses all. All at once and forever! The Mystical Body of Christ is not an institution; it is a reality. That's why I stay in the church: so I can talk with people about it from the place I first learned about it. Right here, right now.

> Hear, O Israel, Adonai is our God, Adonai is One!
> —DEUTERONOMY 6:4

> There is nothing but God. God is the Light of the heavens and the earth.
> —THE QUR'AN

> One perfect nature pervades and circulates within all natures. One all-inclusive Reality contains and embraces all realities. One moon is reflected in every expanse of water. Every reflected moon is one moon. The essence of all Buddhas is in my being. My essence is in their being.
> —YUNG-CHIA TA-SHIH, ZEN MASTER

8

The Communion of Saints

*To be connected with the Church is to be associated with
scoundrels, warmongers, fakes, child-molesters, murderers,
adulterers and hypocrites of every description. It also, at the
same time, identifies you with saints and the finest persons
of heroic soul within every time, country, race, and gender.
To be a member of the church is to carry the mantle of both
the worst sin and the finest heroism of soul because the
church always looks exactly as it looked at the
original crucifixion, God hung among thieves.*
—RONALD ROLHEISER, *THE HOLY LONGING*

And one of those thieves won a ticket to heaven. I love
saints. Not the plaster saints who can do no wrong, but
the real ones who are both larger than life and just like us.

✛ St. Joseph, who no doubt hit the ceiling when his newly
  betrothed told him she was pregnant but who valued
  fidelity so much that he married her anyway and taught
  their Son to carve beauty from beams of wood.

✛ Mary, the mother of Jesus, who emptied herself of ego so she could be filled with the light of the world, who laughed with her toddler, scolded her adult son when he refused to turn water into wine at a wedding feast (he did it her way), and cried as she held him in her arms at the foot of his cross.

✛ Mary Magdalene, the public sinner who washed Jesus' feet with her tears and dried them with her hair, who Jesus lifted and said, "Her sins are forgiven because she loves much" (Luke 7:46). If Mary Magdalene was not at Jesus' side during the Last Supper, you can bet she was one of the women who prepared it. It was she among all the disciples who did not desert Jesus when he was arrested and crucified, and it was she to whom Jesus chose to appear first when he walked out of the tomb.

✛ Hildegard of Bingen (1098–1179), who like so many nuns today could do it all: teach, write, paint, cook, compose music, make medicine, found a religious community, communicate with peasants and kings, and get in hot water from a bishop for burying a sinner in her abbey's cemetery.

✛ Thomas Aquinas (1225–1274), a theologian who ate too much, whom fellow students called a "Dumb Ox," and who wrote the *Summa Theologiae*, which shaped the history of Catholic thought. Now a doctor of the church, Aquinas got into trouble in his day, too, for mining wisdom from the philosophy of a pagan (Aristotle), and for developing a system of thought that did not rely on church authority but on looking at diverse

points of view and letting the truth speak its own name.
Heard that one before?

+ St. Bonaventure (1221–1274), a classmate of Aquinas
who was as different from his friend as Mr. Wizard is
from Stephen Hawking. Bonaventure was a mystic who
wrote some of the most profound books in the treasury of Catholicism. Wouldn't you like to hear the conversations he and Aquinas had as they walked along
the Seine with their schoolbooks, on their way to the
University of Paris? Bonaventure was also named a doctor of the church and is known as the Seraphic Doctor because he was an angel. Did I forget to tell you
that Bonaventure is my favorite saint and that I sign
off many of my e-mails with "Buona Ventura," which
means "Good Luck"?

+ Brother Lawrence (1611–1691), an ordinary guy who
spent forty years cooking hot meals in a monastery kitch-
en but made such an impression on his peers that his few
words of wisdom are memorialized in *Practice of the Presence of God*. "God regards not the greatness of the work,"
he observed, "but the love with which it is performed."

+ St. Alphonsus Liguori (1696–1787) who lived to be
ninety-one, and that's a miracle because he suffered
from a scrupulous conscience. A scrupulous conscience
is a religious form of obsessive-compulsive disorder
in which you can't stop thinking about your sins and
imperfections and feel weighed down with guilt. It is
a side effect of Catholicism poorly taught and is familiar to many Catholics of my generation. Alphonsus

was afflicted with "a thousand frightening fantasies" and spent much of his life developing a spirituality to help others like him. What I love about Alphonsus is that in spite of his mental anguish, he could found the Redemptorist order, become a bishop, write more than one hundred books on theology and spirituality that have been translated into seventy-one languages, and is a model of hope. If you suffer or know someone who suffers from a scrupulous conscience, may I recommend a book called *A Thousand Frightening Fantasies* by Catholic psychologist William Van Ornum. It has a foreword by John Cardinal O'Connor and is one of the most helpful books I've had the *buona fortuna* to publish.

✠ St. Thérèse of Lisieux (1873–1897), who dedicated every moment of her life to relieving the suffering of others in the Mystical Body of Christ. Like Alphonsus, she sometimes tried too hard and, regrettably, spent a long time dying at an early age of tuberculosis, coughing up blood, in constant pain and near despair. But she died feeling the embrace of God's love. During her life Thérèse was a model of kindness to her fellow Sisters, not a few of them tough to live with. She thought of herself as a Little Flower and called her spiritual path the Little Way. "I am only a very little soul," she wrote, "who can only offer very little things to our Lord." Her autobiography *The Story of a Soul* remains a big thing to many readers after one hundred years in print.

These saints all have imperfections. And they are all worth imitating.

Robert Ellsberg, in his magisterial work *All Saints*, writes about saints like these who have been canonized by the church and about others who are equally deserving. "The church makes no pretense," he writes, "that its canon exhausts the number of actual saints. There are count-less men and women whose holiness is recognized by God alone. Along with the 'official saints' they are commemo-rated by the church on November 1, the feast of All Saints." In his 365 reflections on saints, prophets, and witnesses for our time, Robert includes these contemporary heroes:

+ Mohandas Gandhi (1869–1948), the "Great Soul" of India who believed that "an eye for an eye makes the whole world blind" and taught the world to see that nonviolence is the way to peace. "It is not he who says, 'Lord, Lord' that is a Christian," he wrote, "but 'he who does the will of the Lord'—that is a true Christian."

+ Oscar Romero (1917–1980), the archbishop of San Salvador, who comforted the afflicted and afflicted the comfortable with the gospel of Jesus, and in so doing, became the first bishop martyred on the altar since Thomas Becket in 1170. "I am bound, as a pastor," he said, two weeks before his death, "by divine command to give my life for those whom I love, and that is all Sal-vadorans, even those who are going to kill me."

+ Oskar Schindler (1908–1974), the "Righteous Gentile," who escaped his own history by helping more than a thousand Jews escape death during the Holocaust. Nobody knows exactly why Schindler did what he did, but in the movie *Schindler's List*, the Jewish prisoner Itzhak Stern, played by Ben Kingsley, says to Schindler: "This list . . . is an absolute good. The list is life!"

✢ Flannery O'Connor (1925–1964), the bespectacled novelist from Georgia who illuminated glimmers of grace in human darkness. "I write the way I do," she wrote, "*because* (not though) I am a Catholic," and "The only thing that makes the church endurable is that it is somehow the Body of Christ and that on this we are fed."

✢ Mother Teresa of Calcutta (1910–1997) whom critics mocked when she wrote about losing her faith, and who was a saint precisely because she despaired yet still went on. "If you judge people," she once said, "you have no time to love them."

✢ Cardinal Joseph Bernardin (1928–1996), the archbishop of Chicago who presented us with "the seamless garment of life," the understanding that all life, from womb to tomb, is sacred, and who forgave the young man who tried to destroy his life with a false accusation of molestation. "We cannot run away from our family," Bernardin said. "We have only one family, so we must make every effort to be reconciled."

Many of us Catholics stay in the church because it has introduced us to people like these who are larger than life but just like us.

> The saints are the sinners who keep on trying.
> —ROBERT LOUIS STEVENSON

When Therese Borchard and I were writing our book, *I Like Being Catholic*, we wrote to hundreds of people. One of the many responses that didn't make it into the book was this one from our friend Tom Bruce. As the Bible says: "Now is the acceptable time" (2 Corinthians 6:2, NRSV).

> For me personally it's the Communion of Saints. I've been working for the Franciscans for 15 years and had the opportunity to visit Assisi and Rome last year. I am always struck by the nearness of Francis, Anthony, and Clare and other Franciscan saints. This is true of Catholicism as a whole. The Catholic Church is a large dysfunctional family that we all can identify with. You may not like everything about your family but you learn to deal with them. It is the reason Catholics love saints. They are like old—or crazy—aunts and uncles we love and we have known since we were kids. There is a history of 2000 years of seeing how people in the church have tried to follow Jesus—warts and all. They are real people reflecting the culture of their times.

The communion of saints is not just about imitating and loving these folks, it's also about going to them. Listen to this cradle Catholic who knows what he's talking about:

> Catholics have saints—more than 10,000 of them. They're like God's customer service reps, and each of them has a specialty. Say you lose your wallet. You

could bother the Creator to help you find it, but if you're a Catholic, you don't have to. Just pray to St. Anthony. Finding lost things is all he does. Also there are times when you might want to pray to St. Agatha. She's the patron saint of nursing and bell-making. If you're both a nurse and a bell-maker, that's one-stop shopping. (Stephen Colbert in *I Am America*)

Still Catholic? Sure. I've got more than ten thousand reasons to still hang out.

9

There's Still Something about Mary

She is a reflection of eternal light, / a spotless mirror of the working of God, and an image of his goodness.
—WISDOM 7:26, NRSV

In her beautiful book *Mary*, the poet Kathy Coffey reminds us how often Mary must have gazed into the face of her son. Did she look into her baby's eyes and think as all mothers do, *He has my eyes*? Did his laughter ignite her joy? Did his resolve remind her of her purpose? Jesus was the mirror of God, and Mary was a mirror to her son. What she saw was a reflection of God. Isn't that how it is with mothers?

There's something about Mary that still charms us, attracts us, and makes us want to be better women and men.

In Mel Gibson's movie *The Passion of the Christ*, we see the boy Jesus fall down and Mary rush to help him, as any mother would. The movie cuts to Jesus falling under the weight of his cross, and again Mary rushes to help him, as any mother would. As a young man Jesus playfully splashes his mother with water, and they laugh and she chases him in a scene that mirrors a time from our own youth. When Jesus suffers the agony in the garden, his mother wakes from her sleep, sensing his pain as if it were her own. She follows her son on the way of the cross, wiping his blood from the ground after he is scourged, squeezing through the crowds to comfort him, and standing with the disciple John when Jesus says to them from the cross: "Woman, behold your son! Son, behold your mother!"

Catholics do not worship Mary. They honor her, imitate her, and love her—as Jesus did.

Any good mother is worthy of no less.

> *One should honor Mary as she herself wished and as she expressed it in the Magnificat. She praised God for his deeds. How then can we praise her? The true honor of Mary is the honor of God, the praise of God's grace. . . . Mary is nothing for the sake of herself, but for the sake of Christ. . . . Mary does not wish that we come to her, but through her to God.*
> —Martin Luther, Explanation of the Magnificat, 1521

Just like everyone else, whenever we have a need, Vickie and I pray. We hold hands, and one of us takes the lead. If it's me, I talk directly to God for both of us, sort of like: "Dear God, our worries about (*fill in the blank*) are killing us. Please help us to think your thoughts, not our own. Take away our worries, and replace them with your peace. We put this problem on the altar of your love. We know you will take it from us and everything will be okay in your time, not ours. We know your will for us is better than anything we can imagine. Thy will be done. Okay, we're not going to think about this anymore. Thank you,

God." That works pretty well, even though we may have to repeat it later in the day. Now if Vickie takes the lead, we hold hands and it goes exactly like this:

> Our Father who art in heaven, hallowed be thy name. Thy kingdom come, thy will be done, on earth as it is in heaven. Give us this day our daily bread, and forgive us our trespasses as we forgive those who trespass against us. And lead us not into temptation but deliver us from evil. Amen.
>
> Hail Mary, full of grace. The Lord is with thee. Blessed art thou amongst women and blessed is the fruit of thy womb Jesus. Holy Mary, mother of God, pray for us sinners now and at the hour of our death. Amen.

And that works too. Vickie knows from experience: the best way to get to a son is through his mother.

Catholics who feel a bond with Mary know, as Martin Luther did, that when they go to God through Mary, it works. They can't prove it intellectually. They know it through the spiritual fruits that sprout from their prayer: peace, understanding, gratitude. Jesus put it this way: "You will know them by what they produce. People don't pick grapes from thorn bushes or figs from thistles, do they?" (Matthew 7:16, adapted). Catholics go to God through Mary and receive grapes, figs, apples, pears, and sometimes pizza. It works.

Mary's presence in the lives of Catholics—and anyone else who goes to God through her—is the presence of a mother. She is the beat of Jesus' heart. She is a mirror that

shows us who and what we are. The mystic Meister Eckhart
said it best:

> What good is it to me if Mary is full of grace and if
> I am not also full of grace? What good is it to me for
> the Creator to give birth to his Son if I do not also give
> birth to him in *my* time and *my* culture? . . . We are all
> meant to be mothers of God.

10

It's the Stories, Stupid!

*Practically speaking, your religion is the
story you tell about your life.*
—ANDREW GREELEY

I was eight years old and lying next to Gramma Lou on
her beat-up blue sofa that smelled like my dad. My parents were divorced, and Gramma Lou was the harbor I
could always go to, to know that I was safe. Every weekday
when I got off for lunch at St. Andrew's school, I'd walk
through the playground to her house, where she'd make
me a peanut butter-and-jelly sandwich and a cold glass of
Bosco chocolate milk. After lunch we'd lie next to each
other on the sofa and Gramma would read a comic book
to me. Her favorite and mine was *Blackhawk*. Blackhawk
was an ace fighter pilot from World War II who gathered
a motley crew around him to fight injustice. Did I tell you
that my dad was a WWII pilot with more missions than
Catch-22's Yossarian? That he earned two purple hearts
and gave them to me along with his leather fly jacket that
had thirty-two little bombs painted in white on the front?

He also killed Hitler with a penknife, but we won't go there, because nobody believed me then and you may not believe me now, but believe me, it's true. He told me.

That day, lying next to Gramma Lou, I pushed the comic book down with a finger and said, "Mamma Lou, I don't want to go back to school. I want to stay with you."

"We'll see," she said. "Oh, look, Chop-Chop's coming through the window!"

Chop-Chop was Blackhawk's sidekick. He used to be a cook and carried a butcher's cleaver. I pushed the comic down, turned on my side, and looked at Gramma Lou. "Momma Lou," I said, "you love me, don't you?" It was more a statement than a question.

She looked at me with her sweet brown eyes the color of Cracker Jacks. "Of course, I love you."

"Even when I'm bad, right?"

"Yes." She smiled.

"You'll always love me, won't you, Mamma Lou?"

She took me in her arms and said, "Michael, you could take Chop-Chop's hatchet and chop off my arms and chop off my legs and chop off my head and throw them all in a garbage can, and my head would still look at you and tell you again, 'I love you!'"

That was the day I knew everything. Though I didn't know it at the time.

Fast forward ten years. I'm in my room at St. Mary of the Lake Seminary. No blue sofa, just a desk and a chair, a dresser and a bed. I'm reading the Gospel of John. My goal is to read the whole Bible before the end of the year. A line in the first letter of St. John stops the world. "God is love,

and he who lives in love, lives in God, and God in him."
I'm in Mamma Lou's arms again. I know for sure what my
heart knew then: God is all embracing, ever enfolding,
all knowing, ever caring, completely and unconditionally
love! God reads us comic books when we're eight years old
and unlocks the Scriptures when we grow up. Suddenly, I
had a basic premise by which to walk through life: God *is*
love. I am *in* love. Just as nothing could separate me from
the arms of Mamma Lou, nothing will ever separate me
from the love of God!

That is my Catholic story.

You don't have to be Catholic to have a story like this. You
just need a Gramma Lou. But all of my life stories seem
to have a religious dimension, and the religion I grew up
with was all about stories of God: Joseph and his pregnant
wife, Mary, fleeing to Egypt on a donkey from a mad king
who wanted to kill every boy baby in the land, and stopping in a backwater town where Mary gave birth to the
King of kings in the safety of a stable. Don Bosco gather-
ing orphans as an eagle gathers its babies under its wings,
feeding them, sheltering them, and teaching them to fly
again. Joan of Arc, a peasant girl who looked like Ingrid
Bergman and rode a horse and defeated an army, only to
be burned at the stake by a corrupt cardinal for wearing
men's clothing and listening to God's voice and refusing
to tell a lie. The stories of saints, the sagas of sinners, the
rumors of angels! Holy Thursday, Good Friday, Easter!
That's what Catholicism is about!

Does the institutional church have anything to do with all this? Sure. That's why it exists—to tell the stories.

It took four centuries for the church to chisel the doctrine of the Incarnation into a precise statement about the truth, but the story of Jesus, Mary, and Joseph was there from the beginning. Andrew Greeley writes: "It is the story that appeals to the total human. It is the beauty of the story which holds Catholics to their heritage. I'm still a Catholic because of the beauty of the Catholic stories. So are most of us Catholics. Beauty is not opposed to truth. It is simply truth in its most attractive form."

Vickie and I were having pizza the other night with our friends John and Mary Jane Cooke. They asked me what I was writing these days, and I told them I was working on a book about staying Catholic and was on the chapter called "It's the Stories, Stupid!" Mary Jane, a cradle Catholic from Buffalo, got it right away. "You know," she said, "I don't go to church anymore, but I'll always be Catholic. When I had my radiation therapy, I said the rosary every night. It was the stories—the sorrowful mysteries, the joyful mysteries—that helped me get through it. I remember making the stations of the cross when I was a little girl. I loved walking through those stories of Jesus carrying his cross, Veronica wiping his face with her veil, Simon the stranger who helped him when he fell. They're so sad and so hopeful at the same time. I loved reading stories of the saints." There was no stopping her now. "There's such comfort in hearing a story again and again," she said. "Something that doesn't change. Something that makes sense. That's why kids say, 'Tell it to me again. I want to hear it again!' The catechisms told us that Jesus loves us. The stories make it so."

And so it is.

John Shea wrote a book called *Stories of God*. In it he claims that all of us are the stories that God tells himself. And isn't it wonderful that when we go off on the wrong path, God can write straight with crooked lines? Our stories are never over. That's why I stay Catholic—to see what happens next!

11

Jesus Died for Our Sins and Rose from the Dead—*Really!*

Jesus came above all to teach us love.
—POPE JOHN PAUL II, ATTRIBUTED

If I weren't Catholic, I'd still be drawn to Jesus. Anyone who points to the birds of the air and says to his friends, "Don't worry. Look at the sparrows. They don't gather their food into barns. Your heavenly Father takes care of them. Aren't you just as valuable?"—has my attention. Anyone whose only written words were scrawled in the sand and washed away by the rain but whose teachings have changed hearts for two thousand years is worthy of everyone's attention. Anyone who can forgive the brutes who crucified him because he knew that they did *not* know what they were doing makes my hair stand on end.

And yet, a stumbling block for so many people outside the church is the teaching that serves as the church's building block: Jesus died for our sins and rose from the dead. Really? What does that mean?

Get ready for a roller-coaster ride into Aladdin's castle, down corridors of spiritual wonder that the church has ignored for too long!

Why did Jesus die? Whose fault was it? What's it all about, really? Theologians have been trying to answer these questions for centuries. The one whose theology of salvation stuck was Anselm of Canterbury (1033–1109), a man of prayer whose work *Cur Deus Homo* (Why God Became Man) never became a dogma but has influenced the church's teachings about Jesus to this day.

You are familiar with his theory. Adam and Eve, the first man and woman, offended God. That original sin demanded satisfaction. That sin got transmitted to their children and to all children ever since, something like a mutant gene. God could not just forgive Adam and Eve, let alone the human race, because divine mercy of this sort, according to Anselm, "is opposed to God's justice which allows for nothing but punishment to be the return for sin." And man, any man or all men, could not make up for that sin because God is infinite and man is finite. It would take a "God-man" to atone for Adam and Eve's sin and the inherited sin of everyone who didn't choose to be born but were born anyway for millennia to come. So God sent his only Son—innocent, loving, and infinite—to be tortured and killed as a ransom for sinful humanity.

This eleventh-century theory made it all the way to *The Baltimore Catechism* in 1885: "If God forgave us without any satisfaction, His justice would not have been satisfied and we would always feel guilty." Nobody ever asked if the reason Christians feel guilty is because they have learned that their sins nailed God to the cross, and that guilt inevitably leads to more sins and more guilt. Does this theory make sense, really?

How often do we see cynical comics on TV make fun of this vengeful god who sent his only beloved son to a cruel death for all the people who never heard of him before he was born and all those who came after? It's a god who cries out, "I don't get no satisfaction!" and a god whose existence even cradle Catholics are starting to doubt.

Questions beginning with the word *why* (as we saw in chapter 5) often lead to other futile questions and we wind up like snakes chasing our own tail.

Terrence Rynne in his masterful book *Gandhi and Jesus: The Saving Power of Nonviolence* writes:

> The vivid, pulsing, flesh-and-blood life of Jesus of Nazareth, his thrilling words, his arresting personality, his terrible death—the whole of what he did—all turned into a cold, bloodless courtroom scene. And that is to be Good News? It is no wonder that this message of "salvation" has so little appeal or meaning to people today. It is a wonder that this version, this extended metaphor, has endured for so long.

Is it any wonder that so many Catholics, especially Catholics hurt by the church, turn away from a church that promotes this kind of God? Fr. Joseph Ratzinger, now Pope Benedict XVI, in his book *Introduction to Christianity*

(1966) wrote: "One turns away in horror from a righteousness whose sinister wrath makes the message of love incredible."

But wait! I told you we'd be going on an adventure into the deposit of faith that has been forgotten, neglected, or ignored for too long. There is another way of looking at things! St. Anselm, a holy man who sincerely sought truth, may have won a theology contest for the ages but for every first-place winner on *American Idol* or the like, there is always a Clay Aiken. Meet Athanasius (293–373), bishop of Alexandria and doctor of the church!

It was St. Athanasius who taught that Jesus Christ, the Son of God, came into the world and died for us not as a ransom but as a gift to lead all people out of the darkness of the human condition. It was Athanasius, not Shirley MacLaine, who famously said, "God became man so we could become gods." It was Athanasius whom the *Catholic Encyclopedia* calls "the greatest champion of Catholic belief on the subject of the Incarnation that the Church has ever known and [who] in his lifetime earned the characteristic title, Father of Orthodoxy, by which he has been distinguished ever since."

Athanasius lived seven centuries before Anselm, but his simple, positive, and understandable theology of salvation didn't have legs. Neither did the theory of Abelard (1079–1142), who lived in Anselm's time and taught that it was Jesus' love and example—his life, death, and resurrection—that bring us salvation. The deposit of faith fills to overflowing with the ideas of saints and thinkers who glorify love, not fear; harmony, not suffering; and encourage us to experience life eternal, starting now, by coming to know God and Jesus Christ whom he has sent (John 17:3). It is not a God *of* love, but a God who *is* love.

The *Catechism of the Catholic Church* teaches, "The Word became flesh *so that thus we might know God's love*" (italics not mine), and "The Word became flesh *to be our model of holiness*" (ditto), and "to make us *partakers of God's nature.*" What could be more compelling?

How many Catholics who have grown tired of stale old sermons based on atonement theories that not even the pope can tolerate might stay in the church if they heard more about "the good stuff" in the deposit of faith? The "stuff" of which the Bible says each of us is made: *love.*

> If Christ was not raised, then all our preaching is useless, and your trust in God is useless.
> —1 Corinthians 15:14, NLT

Jesus died for our sins and rose from the dead. Really!

And what of the resurrection of Jesus? What really happened? What does it mean?

Did Jesus physically rise from the dead, or is it a myth that points to a truth? The sacramental imagination sings. You can nail love to a cross, but you can't destroy it. "Easter means you can put truth in a grave but it won't stay there" (Clarence Hall). We begin to die the moment we're born, but Jesus gives us new life the moment he dies. Jesus was the greatest spiritual teacher who ever lived. How wonderful to believe he allowed human beings who were wracked with human guilt to scapegoat him and kill him for their fearful sins, to show once and for all that God desires love not sacrifice (Hosea 6:6), and then rose from the dead, literally, as promised, to demonstrate that everything he taught was true!

But is belief enough? Doesn't belief leave room for doubt? Doesn't doubt imply a belief? Carl Jung when asked whether or not he believed in God, answered, "I don't have to believe. I *know.*"

There is a way of knowing that has nothing to do with the brain. We don't look at a cardiogram to see a loving heart any more than we ask for proof that the body needs oxygen before we breathe. Neither do we need a reporter at Bethlehem or a movie of Mary Magdalene at the tomb to know that Christ is born, Christ is risen, and Christ will come again, then and now, in us. There is more to knowing than meets the eye.

"He departed from our sight," wrote Augustine, "so we might return to our heart and there find Him. For he departed, and behold, he is *here.*"

I am learning to experience the Resurrection every time I fall and rise again; every time I sin and know that to God, my scarlet sins are "whiter than snow" (Psalm 51:6); every time I see a brown leaf fall from a tree and know that a new one will be born again.

> Today is the day of salvation for the world. Christ is risen from the dead: arise with him. Christ has come forth from the tomb: free yourselves from the fetters of evil. The gates of hell are open and the power of death is destroyed. The old Adam is superseded, the

new perfected. In Christ a new creation is coming to birth: renew yourselves! —ST. GREGORY OF NAZIANZUS, SECOND ORATION ON EASTER (ADAPTED)

I am still Catholic because the life, death, and resurrection of Jesus are important to me. Are they as important as finding out who will win *Dancing with the Stars* next week? Yes, and that is saying a lot. Are they as important to me as waking up alive tomorrow morning? No, I can't say that. But I'm still here because the church is a good place for me to keep talking with friends about Jesus, even though not as much as we talk about *Dancing with the Stars.* Isn't it amazing how we take the best things in life for granted?

12

The Church Can Change—*Really!*

*To live is to change, and to be perfect
is to have changed often.*
—John Cardinal Newman

The church has changed. The church is changing. The church will change again.

Rules, rituals, and even teachings change all the time. What doesn't change is the chosen part of things, what Hopkins called "the dearest freshness deep down things." What remains the same is beauty, not representations of beauty; truth, not statements about the truth; goodness, not good deeds. The chosen part can never change because it is spiritual.

What often troubles people about the church are the things that don't matter because they are made of matter. Let me explain.

During the first century, Peter and Paul fought over the matter of circumcision. Peter was a Jew, and circumcision was part of his tradition. Paul ministered to the Gentiles and didn't want to force upon them the Jewish law. Their argument split the new church in two. Who was worthy to become a Christian—cut or uncut? Final answer! Their debate was such a big deal that historians memorialized it as the Incident at Antioch, the religious version of *Gunfight at the O.K. Corral.* Did you know that? Of course not. Are you circumcised? Who cares?

Will anyone care two thousand years from now about today's debates? Women priests? Married priests? Who knows? One thing is certain: the expression of priesthood will change by default if not by design. It's no secret: the male celibate priest is a vanishing species. God bless all the good guys—and that is most of them— for their kindness and dedication. But the form will be as different in the future as the Cathedral of Our Lady of the Angels is different from the Cathedral of Cologne, and when the rule does change (in far less than two thousand years), people will wonder what the fuss was all about. They probably won't even know there ever *was* a fuss. The form of priesthood changes. Its chosen part remains the same: service to others for the sake of the kingdom of God.

Rules change. Since "nobody knows when" until 1966, every Catholic who ate meat on Friday went to hell. Those who were born after 1966 did not. Catholics before 1966 believed that rule and its penalty would never change. Now they wonder what happened to the poor bastards who ate a hamburger before the change.

You have to have a sense of humor about the human condition. What doesn't change is the chosen part of fasting: gratitude in place of gratification.

It's not only rules that change; rituals change as well. Did you know that the church never reached a consensus on how many sacraments there are until the thirteenth century? Did you know that Mass was said in the vernacular (native languages) until the Council of Trent in 1563, when the church mandated Latin, until 1965, and then changed it again to the vernacular? Did you know that bishops banned the laity from reading missals for centuries and now are editing the language in the millions of missals they encourage the laity to read?

You have to be patient with the human condition. What doesn't change is the chosen part of liturgy: the grace in the silence between the words.

It's not only rules and rituals that can change; so can teachings. Did you know that from day one until after the Civil War, the church considered slavery morally acceptable, as long as the masters treated their slaves humanely? that Galileo was condemned in 1633 for teaching that the earth revolved around the sun, not the other way around, as the church believed, and that the poor guy wasn't let off the hook until 1992? Did you know that until the twentieth century the church taught sex in marriage to be a necessary evil for the procreation of children?

You have to forgive the human condition. What doesn't change is the chosen part of church history: the opportunity to learn and forgive.

The late, great American bishop Raymond Lucker (1927–2001) of New Ulm, Minnesota, wrote:

> In the past the church made errors and mistakes, not on essential teachings but in reformable statements of the teaching church. It is refreshing to recognize and admit this and to acknowledge that we can grow in our understanding of the message of revelation and in the expression and application of the teaching of the church, given to us by Jesus, to different times and different cultural expressions.

Bishop Lucker had a lifelong interest in learning how to understand the difference between a definitive (unchangeable) church teaching and an authoritative (not unchangeable) teaching. The Incarnation, for instance, is clearly a definitive church teaching. Celibacy of the clergy is not. The right understanding of what is changeable and what is not can lead to a choice between a familiar path and a road less traveled that "makes all the difference" in the life of the people of God. Bishop Lucker identified sixty-four church teachings that have changed throughout history and twenty-two that could change someday because they are not definitive. Those changeable church teachings include birth control, communion of the divorced and remarried, general absolution, intercommunion, and homosexuality.

The church has not only changed throughout the ages, but it has also changed more in the fifty years since Vatican II than in the first two thousand years—just like everything else in the world. The future came yesterday, and the rate of change is the blink of an eye. Today's cell phone is tomorrow's telegraph. Two or three of the authoritative (not unchangeable) teachings of the church are poised to fall like the Berlin Wall, unexpectedly but not surprisingly. Consider birth control. In 1966 a papal commission of seventy-two experts from five continents, including bishops, clergy, physicians, and married couples, after three years of study advised Pope Paul VI that artificial birth control was not intrinsically evil and that Catholic couples should be allowed to decide for themselves what methods to use. But the head of the commission, Cardinal Alfredo Ottaviani, counseled the pope that a change in this teaching would jeopardize the church's credibility. In 1968 the pope issued the encyclical *Humanae Vitae* which reiterated the church's anti-birth-control position. Immediately the church's credibility was in jeopardy. In 2011, eight out of ten Catholics are certain that artificial birth control is a blessing, not a sin. This nondefinitive teaching can change. What will not change is the chosen part of sexual intimacy in marriage: love.

The church has changed. It is changing. It will change.

After the dust settles, the gold will remain.

I value Catholicism because I cherish the chosen part of things. I stay in the church because I want to see what happens next.

13

You Can Disagree with the Church and Still Be a Good Catholic

Years ago on *Saturday Night Live* the actors Billy Crystal and Christopher Guest played Willie and Frankie, two New York pals who are always hurting themselves and sharing their woes with each other. The running line was, "I hate when that happens!"

Willie once told Frankie about the time he took a meat thermometer and shoved it into his ear as far as it would go.

"Boy, that must smart!" Frankie said.

"I know! I hate when that happens!"

Then Frankie told Willie about the time he took a carrot scraper and twisted it up his nose. "I'm getting all the mucus membranes out of there, you know? And then I take one of them, uh—?"

"Mentholated eucalyptus cough drops?"

"Right. And I stick it—wedge it up there, you know? I take a couple of whiffs. Boy! You feel like your head's going to explode!"

"Right. I hate when that happens!"

You know when I feel like my head is going to explode? When I'm watching a cable talk show and two Catholics are arguing about the church and one of them tells the other: "You're not Catholic! You can't say that and still be Catholic. Why don't you just join another church?" I hate when that happens!

The person who makes that statement hurts the other and by so doing hurts himself and everybody else. He's Willie sticking a pencil in his eye and encouraging Frankie to walk on tacks. Remember when we talked about the Mystical Body of Christ in chapter 7?

> There are many parts but only one body. The eye cannot say to the hand, "I don't need you!" And the head cannot say to the feet, "I don't need you!" On the contrary, those parts of the body that seem to be weaker are indispensable, and the parts that we think are less honorable we treat with special honor. If one part suffers, every part suffers with it. If one part is honored, every part rejoices with it. Now you are the body of Christ, and each one of you is a part of it! (1 Corinthians 12:20–27, NIV)

We can no more remove ourselves from the body of Christ than we can separate ourselves from our own body. The calmest answer to the challenge to leave I ever heard was from Fr. Andrew Greeley years ago on *The Phil Donahue*

Show when a woman asked him, "If you disagree with the church, why don't you just leave?"

"Because I like being Catholic."

Fr. Greeley would later famously say, "Even if they throw me out, I won't go." Indeed, the only way to leave the church is to say so yourself. The church's harshest penalty, excommunication, forbids a Catholic from receiving the sacraments until he repents; it doesn't turn anyone into an unbaptized Catholic. Catholicism is in your spiritual DNA; it traces back to a pool of blood at the foot of the cross. You can't wash it off.

The Catholic response to an individual who disagrees on a nondefinitive church teaching (as we saw in chapter 11 many of the controversial ones are open to question) is to participate with them in a mutual search for clarity. We belong to one body and cannot cut off a member without hurting the whole body. "In essentials, unity," wrote John XXIII, "in doubtful matters, liberty; and in all things, charity." The essential, of course, *is* charity. Too bad that charity doesn't make for good TV.

Not surprisingly, many of these debates are really about politics, not religion. Can a governor who supports the law on *Roe v. Wade* receive communion? Can a Supreme Court justice who rules against the church's teaching on capital punishment still call himself Catholic? And what's up with the Catholic commentators who support the church's teaching on sex and in the same breath say the pope and bishops don't know what they're talking about on issues of economics and social justice? The arguments are more about being a Democrat or a Republican than being a Catholic or a heretic.

Yet how many Catholics stop being Catholic because they cannot in conscience agree with the church on issues such as birth control and get the idea that it doesn't behoove them to stay? How many other Catholics are hanging on to the ship of the church by their fingernails because they've heard that dissent is akin to mutiny? Add to that the scandals and the undernourishing sermons, and it's a wonder that most Catholics still say with Andrew Greeley, "Even if you throw me out, I'm not leaving. It's my church too!"

A Benedictine monk of fifty years, Philip Kaufman wrote a helpful book called *Why You Can Disagree and Remain a Faithful Catholic*. He first points out that a Catholic, like any intelligent human being, has a responsibility to "follow a sincerely informed conscience. That doesn't mean that we can do whatever we please. It does mean that once we have made an honest effort to determine what we should do or avoid doing, we have an obligation to act according to that conviction."

As Pope John Paul II put it in *The Splendor of Truth*: "The judgment of conscience has an imperative character: man must act in accordance with it."

Today it is easier than ever to have an informed conscience. People cannot only read, but they are also more educated—and they can google. All you have to do is google "Birth Control Encyclical" or "Birth Control Catholic" or "Papal Birth Control Commission," and you'll know as much about (if not more than) that issue in less than an afternoon (and from every point of view) as your parish priest. (Sorry, guys, but you know it's true.) Your conscience will tell *you*—you won't tell it—what makes sense for you.

And then you'll be able to go on TV and discuss the church and go home knowing that no matter what anybody says, you *are* a good Catholic!

"I like it when someone tells me they don't agree," says Pope Francis. "This is a true collaboration."

Dissent doesn't make someone an ill-informed Catholic; disinterest does.

I'm still here because these things interest me tremendously, and I'm still Catholic because I'm still learning.

14

The Bethlehem Principle (There Is Room in the Church for Everyone or There Is Room for No One)

The church is a house with 100 gates; and no two men enter at exactly the same angle.
—G. K. CHESTERTON

Way back when, I helped write a business plan for the new Crossroad Publishing Company. Crossroad was a small religious book publisher with strong Catholic roots. As I wrote, a principle wrote itself. I called it the Bethlehem Principle. It went like this:

> There must be room in Crossroad—as there is in the church—for everyone. Two thousand years ago there was no room at the inn for a carpenter and his pregnant wife. And look who they turned out to be! To exclude anyone is to exclude everyone. To give voice to the voiceless is to raise a "shout for joy and gladness" (Psalm 35:27). To move forward is to take risks.

James Joyce famously said, "Catholicism means here comes everybody!" Crossroad means there is a place for Catholics on the left side of the road, the right side, and especially the middle where most Catholics are stumbling toward Bethlehem.

We went on to publish every pope and every theologian a pope would admonish; we made public the ideas of Cardinal Ratzinger before and during his tenure as Prefect for the Congregation of the Faith, as well as the Catholics he questioned; we published the biography of Mother Angelica and the story of Patty Crowley and her adventure on the Papal Birth Control Commission. Most of all we published everybody in-between: Henri Nouwen, Joyce Rupp, folks whose words have nourished Catholics for decades. They are all, each of them, Catholic, and each of them has words and stories that can benefit us all.

And guess what? Nobody ever kicked any of those folks out of the church. They can't.

Somehow, despite the rhetoric, we all *know*: there is room in the church for everyone, or there is room for no one.

There is room in the church for every pope and for everyone he corrects and for everyone who corrects him; for members of Call to Action and followers of Opus Dei; for those who receive communion on the pillow of their tongue and for those who prefer the cup of their palm; for those who save their money for a pilgrimage to Medjugorje and for those who blow it at Vegas; for sinners, saints, and fools.

Too many Catholics fall away from the church because they think there is no room for them. Now more than ever the church must shout out that there *is* room in the inn for everyone. This is not merely a publishing principle— it's the way it is!

Most of all, the church must make space for those it has hurt. "In my Father's house," Jesus said, "there are many dwelling places" (John 14:2, NRSV). Would not Jesus, if he were here today, prepare a great room, a family room of enormous comfort, for victims of abuse, for gay and lesbian Catholics, for divorcees, and for Catholic thinkers who seek to shed light but too often receive only heat in return? If there is not room for everyone, the church is not a home but a country club.

Thomas Merton wrote in *Raids on the Unspeakable*: "[Christ's] place is with those who do not belong, who are rejected by power because they are regarded as weak, those who are discredited, who are denied the status of persons. . . . In these He hides Himself, for whom there is no room."

What the church finds when it follows the example of Jesus is that those who have the biggest wounds are the biggest lovers. Listen to Italian writer Carlo Carretto (1910–1988):

> How much I must criticize you, my church, and yet how much I love you! You have made me suffer more than anyone, and yet I owe more to you than to anyone. I should like to see you destroyed, and yet I need

your presence. You have given me much scandal, and yet alone have made me understand holiness.

Never in this world have I seen anything more compromised, more false, yet never have I touched anything more pure, more generous, or more beautiful. Countless times I have felt like leaving you, my church; and yet every night I have prayed that I might die in your warm, loving arms!

Jesus calls us all to a great feast whose tables are set for everyone: "the poor, the crippled, the blind, and the lame"—and there is still room for more! (Luke 14:15–24)

Catholicism means throwing a party for everyone. We need someone to remind us that the church is a family. Dissent doesn't break up families; disinterest does.

The church as family fills its table to bursting for prodigal sons and daughters—morning, noon, and night. Like the parent in that parable, such a church refuses to condemn or even compare one family member to another. It takes Jesus' word to heart: "Do not judge, and you will not be judged. Do not condemn, and you will not be condemned. Forgive, and you will be forgiven" (Luke 6:36–38, NIV). Or better yet, "My child, you are always with me, and everything I have is yours!" (Luke 15:31, adapted)

I am still Catholic because the story of Bethlehem teaches me we are all welcome. I stay in the church because I know this is true no matter what anybody says.

15

A Dizzying Array of Images for the Church

Understanding means seeing that the same thing said different ways is the same thing.
—LUDWIG WITTGENSTEIN

So what is the Catholic Church anyway? Is it the same as Catholicism? What does the church think it is? What do you mean by *it?*

The church has defined itself over the centuries as the Mystical Body of Christ (my favorite), the bride of Christ, the family of God, the people of God, the temple of the Holy Spirit, and many other beautiful metaphors founded on a spiritual reality.

There are many ways to define the same word. Just as we call the United States a country, a community, a beacon, a pioneer, and a protector, we can define the church as an institution, a mystical communion, a sacrament, a herald, and a servant. What a dizzying array of images! Every metaphor points to a chosen part of Catholicism.

I first knew church as a redbrick building with twin spires on the corner of Addison and Paulina streets in Chicago. I soon knew it as St. Andrew's parish. It was the place where I first learned about Jesus. I also learned how to fight and how to get out of fighting, but maybe that's another story. What made St. Andrew's *church* was not that its spires pointed to heaven but that its flawed people—priests, sisters, parishioners—embodied the mystery of the metaphors: mystical body, family of God, sacrament, servant. Poised between heaven and earth where the visible reaches for the invisible, St. Andrew's was at once a scary place and a sacred place. It was a place on earth where blades of grass could break through cracks in the pavement. Without its spiritual foundation St. Andrew's would be just a pile of bricks. With it, it was a place where we could begin to learn that we are not alone but are members of God's family.

Later in life I would learn through the study of meta-psychiatry that each of us is a "place" where God reveals himself. Having learned in seminary that God is unconditional love, I could put one and one together and understand that my purpose in life is to be a place where love reveals itself. I could also now see how two and two equal church: a place where God reveals himself through members of a community learning to love one another as Jesus did. "Where two or three are gathered in my name, I am there among them" (Matthew 18:20, NRSV).

The Catholic Church is St. Andrew's parish. Only bigger.

Martin Sheen is an actor by profession, but he speaks the wisdom of a theologian. The church is a spiritual community learning to see with Jesus' eyes. Jesus asks the members of his mystical body to participate in God's mission of love and forgive-

> It doesn't really matter how much of the rules or the dogma we have accepted and live by if we're not really living by the fundamental creed of the Catholic Church, which is service to others and finding God in ourselves and then seeing God in everyone— including our enemies.
>
> —MARTIN SHEEN

ness. The church is all about beholding God's presence and action and spreading God's reign that began before the beginning and will have no end.

A wonderful old Maryknoll priest, John Walsh, likes to say, "Church doesn't have a mission. Mission has a church." Pope Benedict XVI has often said, "The church talks too much about structures and not enough about God." God's mission is to turn the world inside out so that we can see the kingdom that is within us (Luke 17:21) and manifest it in our lives. It is a spiritual kingdom of love, reconciliation, and healing.

We don't have to trek across the Himalayas or take a boat down the Amazon or jeep through Africa to extend God's kingdom to all nations (Matthew 28:19). We can do mission by *being* mission on the spot where we are standing. The kingdom of God is spiritual, and so it has no boundaries. It spreads from one corner of the earth to the other "in the twinkling of an eye" (1 Corinthians 15:52).

An eager friar told St. Francis that he couldn't wait to leave the cloister and spread the gospel to the world. Francis smiled and said, "We must preach the good news at all times. If necessary, we use words."

The mission is our everyday lives.

Catholic missiologist Stephen Bevans, SVD, teaches that we are most church not when we are putting mortar on bricks or adding members to a roster but when we are outside of church: "being good parents, being loving spouses, being diligent and honest in our workplace, treating our patients with care if we are health workers, going the extra mile with our students if we are teachers, living lives responsible to the environment, being responsible citizens, sharing our resources with the needy, standing up for social justice, treating immigrants fairly, trying to understand people of other faiths."

We learn, too, that just as we don't have to be Jewish to believe in one God, we don't have to be Catholic to manifest the kingdom of God. The Muslim in Morocco, the Buddhist in Kyoto, the Christian in Kenya are not rivals but allies, companions, and friends on our common journey home. Clement of Alexandria wrote in the first century: "There is but one river of truth, but many streams pour into it from this side and from that." *The Catechism of the Catholic Church* in the twentieth century teaches that "all religions bear witness to men's essential search for God." Religions are different, but God's mission is one. All of us "live and move and have our being in God," and the purpose of life is to come to see that truth so that our lives, not our religions, can be in harmony.

To understand that the church is here for mission has practical implications. "Imagine," writes Bevans, "what the structure of the church would be like if we recognized that it is mission that needs to be first, and not the church. Ministry would exist for the mission and not for itself. So many things that bog us down today would simply fall away: clerical privilege, restrictions on lay people's ministry, the role of women in the ministry and decision making in the church. What would be important is not people's roles in the *church*, but how ministers might equip people for ministry in the world."

There is a dizzying array of images for the church. But the chosen part is clear: It is *us*. And we are here for *God*.

The church is a spiritual community that participates in the saving, healing, and forgiving work of Jesus Christ whom God has sent. The church is you and me and everyone else being Christ to our brothers and sisters in Christ, on the spot where we're standing, and in all places and at all times.

"I see the church as a field hospital after battle," says Pope Francis. "It is useless to ask a seriously injured person if he has high cholesterol and about the levels of his blood sugar. You have to heal his wounds. Then we can talk about everything else!"

We are the place where Jesus and the Father dwell. That is our purpose: to be what we already are.

And that is why I stay in the church. It is where I am.

16

A Mass of Energy

It is no longer I who live, but it is Christ who lives in me.
—Galatians 2:20, NRSV

*Going to Mass does not mean that we shall be filled with
warm feelings for other members of the congregation.
Probably not! But it does imply a gradual transformation of
who I am—"I and no longer I"—discovering God and myself
in the stranger, and God in the core of my being. . . .
The slow working of grace will free me to be sent at
the end. Why go to church? To be sent from it.*
—Timothy Radcliffe, OP, *Why Go to Church?*

The church was dark. It was six-thirty on a winter morning
and there wasn't enough sun to brighten the stained-glass
window in front of the altar. I was serving Mass for an old
priest who faced a marble cross hanging beneath the window. He leaned over a round piece of bread as thin as a
holy card and whispered, "*Hoc . . . est . . . enim . . . corpus . . .
meum!*" I jangled bells welded together like a three-leaf clo-
ver three times. Father genuflected and raised the body of

Christ high in the air. Behind us a handful of women and
men bowed their heads and tapped their breasts three
times. Another morning. Another Mass. Another miracle
to start the day.

I rarely missed daily Mass until I was twenty-eight years
old. I went from being an altar boy to being a teenage semi-
narian. Then from ages twenty-five to twenty-eight I pre-
sided at Mass as a priest. I left the priesthood when I was
twenty-eight to marry. Vickie and I went to Mass every week,
and I sometimes went to a noon mass on my lunch hour in
the city. We were active in our parish, took our boys to Mass
every Sunday, and taught them the faith. The boys never
much liked church, and as they grew up stopped going to
Mass. That bothered Vickie. Not me. They were, as we both
knew, wonderful, kind young men with strong values. I
understood. I was finding it a chore to go to church myself.
The sermons were dreadful. Hardly anyone in the pews
said the prayers or sang the hymns, including me. None
of this was anything new, but for the first time I started
to skip Sundays. Today Vickie still goes every week, and I
attend irregularly. Only four out of ten Catholics, according to a 2008 study by the Center for Applied Research in
the Apostolate (CARA), attend Mass regularly. For the first
time in American religious history, more Protestants go to
church on Sunday than Catholics. Most Catholics do not
believe that missing Mass is a sin. Other surveys show that
only a third of Catholics believe that the bread and wine
become the body and blood of Christ, while two-thirds say
they are just symbolic reminders of Jesus.

Writing this chapter brings me up short. The Eucharist is at the heart of Catholicism, and I'm not that interested anymore. What have I forgotten? What do I need to know? What can I write that is true, honest, and helpful? What is the chosen part of the Mass, the spiritual part that is so clear that I cannot escape its light?

The Mass is a drama in three acts (offertory, consecration, and communion), but it is not a theater piece. If we are looking for entertainment, we're better off going to the movies. The Eucharist is a spiritual happening but not a magic trick. If we're looking for magic,

This teaching is difficult; who can accept it?
—JOHN 6:60

The Eucharist is a mystery not because it is mysterious, but because it is a sign of God's secret purpose, which is to unite all things in Christ.
—TIMOTHY RADCLIFFE,
WHY GO TO CHURCH?

we watch David Copperfield. The Mass seems to take forever but is even longer: "God's gifts are given through the slow transformation of who we are," writes Fr. Radcliffe, "God's undramatic, noiseless work, recreating us as people who have faith, hope, and charity." The energy of the Eucharist is not automatic. We know too many people who have received communion for decades and are still miserable. The invitation to Eucharistic grace comes with an RSVP. The energy of Mass is equal to our willingness to empty our egos.

Just what is this mystery called Eucharist?

The Eucharist is a sacrament, a symbol, a reality, a sacrifice, a reminder, a remembrance, a meal, a thanksgiving, an invitation, and a gift.

Let's break it down.

As a sacrament, Eucharist is at once symbol and reality. The Catholic novelist Flannery O'Connor famously said, "If it's [just] a symbol, to hell with it." No symbol is just a symbol. A symbol is a thing we can see, hear, taste, or touch that represents a reality that is invisible and intangible yet equally present. Every word we speak is a symbol. When we promise "to love and to cherish" in marriage, the words point to a commitment and covenant beyond words. Words are powerful. They are powerful because they stand for something even more powerful and no less real. Eucharist stands for—and really is—the presence of Christ in our lives.

The Eucharist reminds us that Jesus Christ, the Son of God, came into the world to show us that we, too, are born of God, to teach us to love ourselves and to love everyone as he loved us, as brothers and sisters in Christ. It is a remembrance that Jesus made a singular sacrifice to stop all scapegoating once and for all, to end all sacrifice of innocent victims to an angry God and instead to know him as *Abba* (Daddy) and accept his gift of love as did the prodigal son, who had forgotten, and then remembered, who he was and that he could never really leave home. The Eucharist is a remembrance of our salvation that takes place now and always and—how wonderful!—cannot be reversed.

The Eucharist is a spiritual meal. It is not an actual meal any more than the sacrament of baptism is a bath. It isn't chewing on Jesus' flesh but on his teachings. It isn't drinking his corpuscles but his life. We get hung up on the doctrine of transubstantiation by asking *how*. It took the Council of Trent six years (1545–1551) to define that word, and scholars are still debating the details. All we need to know is *what*. "I am the bread of life. Whoever comes to me will never be hungry, and whoever believes in me will never be thirsty" (John 6:35, NRSV). In Eucharist we partake of the Wisdom of God. Fr. Radcliffe writes in *Why Go to Church?*:

> So when we eat the body of Jesus and drink his blood, it is not as if we were to roast our local bishop and devour him at a parish picnic. We are accepting the gift of the one who is Wisdom Incarnate. God's Wisdom is not just a divine intelligence. Wisdom was with God when the world was created, and made it to be our home.

In Eucharist we give thanks for the gift of knowing we have never left Eden, never left home. Jesus comes to assure us that Abba is still with us. Eucharist is an invitation to consume the truth of our being. To be one with Jesus and everyone everywhere who is, in truth, also within us as we are in them and all of us are in the Father. Perhaps the most important words of the Mass are the very last spoken:

"The Mass is ended, go in peace to love and serve the Lord."
"Thanks be to God!"

The Latin words are, literally, "Go, this is your mission!" Our mission is to go out and be like Jesus who has come to us again. The Eucharist is not just a symbol and not just about Sunday; it's about the presence of Christ on Monday and about remembering who we are in the mystical body of Christ.

I'm still Catholic because I keep forgetting what's really important and need reminders. The Eucharist is a reminder and a remembering, an invitation and a gift. I'm pretty sure I'll go to church more frequently than when I did before writing this chapter. Thanks be to God.

17

A Garden of Spiritual Paths

There is not, and never has been, a single Christian spirituality, nor a single Catholic spirituality.
—RICHARD P. McBRIEN, CATHOLICISM

It was just a local cable show, but the other guest called me a "supermarket Catholic," and I got emotional. "So what's so bad about that?" I said. "The Catholic Church is the greatest spiritual supermarket the world has ever known! It has aisles that never end and its spiritual fruits are enough to nourish you for eternity—not to mention the meats, potatoes, and vegetables! No one can eat everything at once. The problem is that the church is promoting only a small portion of what's available in its spiritual storehouse, and a lot of people are hungry for what's been hidden, including the infinite variety of desserts!"

That'll teach him.

The term "supermarket Catholic" soon devolved into "cafeteria Catholic," another derogatory term used to divide allegedly picky Catholics from those who simply eat what is put on their plates. But I stand by my outburst. The

Catholic Church is not only a spiritual supermarket but is a garden of spiritual paths that go in unexpected directions but always lead back to the fountain of life at its center. Fruit trees line every path and the oranges and pears and peaches are always in reach. When it comes to spirituality, the Catholic Church is a Garden of Eden!

Yes, I get carried away.

> If God can work through me, he can work through anyone.
> —FRANCIS OF ASSISI

> If [a man] wishes to be sure of the road he travels on, he must close his eyes and walk in the dark.
> —JOHN OF THE CROSS, *DARK NIGHT OF THE SOUL*

> Run, jump, shout and do whatever you like as long as you don't sin.
> —DON BOSCO

The garden was planted through the centuries by spiritual masters such as St. Francis, St. Benedict, and many others who founded various religious communities. And for centuries discerning Catholics have followed their paths, each one different, each one packed with the same rich soil. They have experienced the earthy joy of the Franciscans, the simplicity of the Cistercians, the compassion of the Little Sisters of the Poor. Some choose to stay on the straight and narrow with the rule of the Benedictines; others elect to circle the globe with Maryknoll missioners. Many like to taste the sweet mysticism of the Carmelites, while others bite into the preaching of the Dominicans. Catholics build themselves up with the spiritual exercises of the Jesuits, and enjoy small pleasures with the playful Salesians. The simple appeal of these founders speaks through the centuries.

Let nothing disturb you,
Let nothing frighten you,
All things are passing away,
God does not change.
Patience obtains all things
Whoever has God lacks nothing;
God alone is enough.

—TERESA OF ÁVILA

Each religious order has a unique way of seeing life from a spiritual perspective that is just right for someone. And the good thing is, you don't have to give up everything, leave home, and become a sister, brother, or priest to adapt their path in your own life.

The number of women and men who live in consecrated religious communities is decreasing as their age increases, but the number of laypeople who are expressing the same spiritual charism in their lives is multiplying like loaves and fishes. Catholics are doing their homework and are not only familiar with the garden of spiritual paths but find themselves attracted to one or more of them. They get up and feed their kids and go to work and eat out with their friends and, at the same time, endeavor to express a spirituality that is proven and appealing.

Some actually attach themselves to a particular religious order or society without ever leaving home. Franciscans, Carmelites, and Dominicans call them "seculars." The Jesuits and Maryknoll Fathers and Brothers call them "affiliates." The Benedictines call them "oblates." They live in cities or suburbs or rural areas far away from the abbey or monastery or motherhouse but walk the spiritual path in their daily lives.

Catharine Henningsen, an accomplished journalist, has been an associate of the Sisters of the Sacred Heart for most of her adult life. As I write this, she is taking care of Sister Margaret Hayes, a Sacred Heart sister and former psychiatrist in her early eighties, at her home in Connecticut. Catharine doesn't do this as part of her role as an associate but because she has a habit of being loving. This is what it means to Catharine to be an associate of the Sacred Heart:

> The charism of the Society—"to show forth the love of the heart of Christ"—has always been highly attractive to me. Now, with Margaret here, I find myself learning more each day about what it means to live it. Margaret's physical hardships now may be great, but it never stops her from getting the loving part right.
>
> Our foundress, St. Madeleine Sophie Barat, is credited with saying, "for a single child I would have founded the Society." I like to think of the "single child" in each person I meet and to ask myself would I give all-in-all for that one person? What I come to, thinking that way, is another of the Society's great spiritual lessons: the practice of being fully present to each one. There are so many paths to finding Christ in the other, but Sophie's is the voice I hear.

Ronnie Gilligan is a Maryknoll affiliate from Long Island who leaves home for three months each year to help missioners. She's been to Thailand, Nepal, Cambodia, Bolivia, Albania, and recently St. Stephen's Mission Church at the Wind River Indian Reservation in Wyoming, where she taught religious education, brought communion to the sick, and "shoveled snow and horse manure." Ronnie writes in *Maryknoll* magazine:

> My association with Maryknoll has helped put words to my beliefs that we don't have to teach God because God is already there. Our job is to help people recognize God in themselves. One night with the family I was preparing for First Communion, the topic came up about what Jesus looked like. Thinking about where the historical Jesus lived and that he and his family were frequently in the sun in the deserts, with no mention of peeling skin or freckles, we concluded that Jesus probably looked more like my Native American hosts than like me.
>
> By night's end we were talking about prayer and where we find God. "God lives in me and I'm Indian," said one of the children. I will remember that for a long, long time.

Few of us have the kind of commitment that Catharine and Ronnie do. But not only do we not have to become a religious to follow a traditional spiritual path, we don't even have to become an associate or an affiliate. We can follow an established path all on our own. That's what a large number of Catholics do. John Michael Talbot, founder of the Brothers and Sisters of Charity, writes in his book *The World Is My Cloister*:

> For every person who joins up as an oblate, secular, domestic or associate, there are hundreds, perhaps even thousands more who find inspiration from simply reflecting on the monastic saints and movements. This is a totally indefinable and innumerable group of folks just trying to make it through the day without totally losing their spiritual footing or perhaps just now finding it. They are Catholics and non-Catholics, Christians and non-Christians, believers and unbelievers. In a way this new phenomenon is a new Pentecost, an event of the Holy Spirit firing people's desire for God.

So just as you don't have to be Catholic to manifest the reign of God, you don't have to be Catholic to walk in the garden of spiritual paths. I like to play on all of them. A lot of us are still Catholic simply because we need the exercise. It's even better than a supermarket.

18

Fruits of the Spirit

Truth is what works.
—WILLIAM JAMES

The proof of the pudding is the eating.
—DON QUIXOTE

*But the fruit of the Spirit is love, joy, peace, patience,
kindness, generosity, faithfulness, gentleness, and
self-control. There is no law against such things.*
—GALATIANS 5:22, NRSV

*The Christian ideal has not been tried and found wanting.
It has been found difficult and left untried.*
—G. K. CHESTERTON, *WHAT'S WRONG WITH THE WORLD*

Well, you've just read the whole chapter. You can move on now.

Still here? Okay, here is how it breaks down.

If a tree on the spiritual path bears good fruit, it's a good tree. The fruits that fall on a valid spiritual path are love, joy, peace, patience, kindness, goodness, faithfulness, gentleness, and discipline. If you experience these spiritual qualities, you are on the right spiritual path for you and can do no wrong. If you experience fear, anger, and joylessness, it's time to consider a road not taken. But before you do, it's wise to ask yourself, *Have I given the trail I'm on a fair trial? Did I study the map at the beginning and along the way?* Most folks stray from the church because other Catholics have given them a bogus map or led them astray by their example. Who can blame them for taking a road trip? All this book suggests is that it wouldn't hurt to "give peace a chance"—the "peace that is beyond all understanding" (Philippians 4:7)—before laying cement over the paths of spirituality Catholicism has to offer. If those fruits of love, joy, and peace still don't manifest, then it's time to go exploring.

At times like this it's beneficial to look at other spiritual paths without abandoning our own. When we study other traditions, we often find our own spirituality enhanced. But that happens only when we're as interested in rediscovering the chosen part of our own religion as we are the chosen part in another. We embrace the baby before we throw out the bathwater. We don't give up the ship even if we're hanging on to the bark of Peter with our fingernails. Maybe a new wind will come along and blow us in a better direction. The breezy immediacy of Eastern spirituality has enriched my appreciation of Catholicism, and Catholic spirituality has led me to appreciate Eastern wisdom. My friend Jack Shea likes to joke about our seminary days, "While everybody else was reading Aquinas, Mike was studying Zen." I read

Aquinas, all three volumes. I just thought Basho was a better poet. Many Catholics today who are frustrated with the church choose to study Buddhism and Zen Masters much more than they do the spiritual teachings of Jesus and the saints. It doesn't make sense to turn our back on fruits that nourish us. When we sincerely look at both trees, we see lovely parallels:

✛ "Your everyday mind—that is the way." Wu-men
✛ "God is found among the pots and pans." St. Thérèse of Lisieux
✛ "Let the children come to me for theirs is the kingdom of heaven." Jesus (Matthew 19:14)
✛ "Children get to heaven by playing." Zen saying
✛ "Overcome anger with love, overcome evil with good, overcome the miser by giving, overcome the liar with truth." Buddha
✛ "Love your enemies, do good to those who hate you, bless those who curse you, pray for those who abuse you. From anyone who takes away your coat do not withhold even your shirt. Give to everyone who begs from you; and if anyone takes away your goods, do not ask for them again." Jesus (Luke 6:27–31)
✛ "The thief left it behind / the moon / at my window!" Ryokan
✛ "If we could see the miracle of a single flower clearly, our whole life would change." Buddha
✛ "Look at the lilies of the field!" Jesus (Matthew 6:28)
✛ "Every moment comes to us pregnant with a command from God, only to pass on and plunge into eternity, there

to remain forever what we have made of it." St. Francis de Sales

✛ "If you walk, just walk. / If you sit, just sit. / But whatever you do, don't wobble." Unmon

✛ "If you do not tend for one another, then who is there to tend for you? If you wish to tend for me, tend the sick. Consider others as yourself." Buddha

✛ "I tell you the truth, whatever you did for one of the least of these brothers of mine, you did for me. . . . Do unto others as you would have them do unto you." Jesus (Matthew 25:40 and Matthew 7:12)

Now, to paraphrase my friend John Lennon, who got in trouble for saying the Beatles were more popular than Jesus and then had to apologize; I'm not saying that Buddhism is more popular than Catholicism or Catholicism is better or both are equal. I'm only saying there are lovely expressions of truth everywhere, and if one bears good fruit for you, it is valid. If it doesn't, hey, that's okay too. "Road trip!"

Can we know for sure that we are on the right spiritual path? Is it enough to believe that God said it was the right path? That works for many people. But since you're reading this book—and I hope you've rediscovered a lot of treasures stored in the attic of Catholic consciousness so far—that may not be working all that well for you. After all, belief implies doubt, just as doubt depends on belief. We can't say "I believe" without confirming the possibility of doubt. How can we *know* a spiritual path is valid for us?

Jesus put it very simply; he said: "By their fruits you shall know them" (Matthew 7:20). Further, he said, "When you know the truth, it will make you free" (John 8:32).

We *can* know whether or not an idea is spiritually valid in our lives. We don't have to take somebody else's word for it. We don't have to read a Gallup poll or watch Dr. Phil or leave our experiences at the door of the church. We don't have to agree or disagree with anyone. We have only to consider if there is more love, joy, peace, patience, kindness, goodness, faithfulness, gentleness, and discipline in our lives than there was before. Now that may or may not happen right away, and nobody is going to be spiritually awake and aware all the time. But it will happen if we are sincere in our spiritual search.

Ralph Waldo Emerson said, "Life is a journey, not a destination." So did Aerosmith. It must be true. Jesus was stronger: "I am the Way, the Truth, and the Life" (John 14:6). The way is a journey among trees that bear good fruit. The tree is valid not because it is true; it is true because it bears good fruit. How many of us have taken the time to understand what Jesus meant when he said those words? Before we leave something, it's a good idea to understand, on our own, what it is we are leaving.

I'm still Catholic because Catholicism as I've grown to understand it over the years brings me love, joy, peace, patience, kindness, goodness, faithfulness, gentleness, and discipline. I stay in the church even as it drives me nuts, like my family of birth, because it's been a good home for me and I can always take road trips and come back revived, and be grateful for the spiritual garden I never really left, with its abundant fruits that always stay fresh.

19

The Seamless Garment of Life

When the soldiers crucified Jesus, they took his clothes,
dividing them into four shares, one for each of them,
with Jesus' cloak remaining. This garment was seamless,
woven in one piece from top to bottom.
—JOHN 19:23

When Chicago's Cardinal Bernardin was dying of cancer, Chicagoans responded as they did when they heard
that President Roosevelt had died. The announcement
brought the city of broad shoulders to its knees. The
Tribune quoted the cardinal as saying he faced death with
peace and that it was a gift from God.

Jeremy Langford, a young editor from Loyola Press,
was working with the cardinal on a memoir that after
Bernardin's death would become the inspirational bestseller *The Gift of Peace.* Jeremy asked the cardinal, "Did I
misunderstand what you said to the press? Was the gift
from God knowing when you are going to die or the sense
of peace?" The cardinal smiled and answered, "Many

people misunderstood. It's interesting, isn't it? We can understand cancer but peace is less comprehensible."

After his death not only Chicagoans but Catholics everywhere would remember Joseph Bernardin for teaching us how to die with dignity. Few would remember how he taught a whole world to live with dignity through his profoundly Catholic idea, the Seamless Garment of Life. Isn't it interesting? We can understand the inevitability of death, but the sanctity of life is less comprehensible.

Here is Cardinal Bernardin's gift to the world.

It is not a belief but a *knowing* that all of us are one. The Seamless Garment of Life is not a theory but a principle that all life is sacred, from womb to tomb, in the unborn and the dying, in the murderer on death row and the mother in a coma, in the soldier in Afghanistan and the homeless family in Iraq, in the child abused by a pedophile and the pensioner who can't afford a doctor, in the oil-poisoned Gulf and the coal mines of Pennsylvania, in the Arab and in the Israeli. "When human life is considered 'cheap' or easily expendable in one area," said Cardinal Bernardin, "eventually nothing is held as sacred and all lives are in jeopardy."

Sister Eileen Egan (1911–2000), a cofounder of the peace organization Pax Christi, coined the phrase *seamless garment of life* in 1973. A decade later Bernardin (1928–1996) turned the metaphor into a consistent ethic of life. It became a cloak of moral issues woven together as seamlessly as Jesus' tunic and was an endeavor to bring unity to Catholic teaching. He wrote:

If one contends, as we do, that the right of every fetus to be born should be protected by civil law and supported by civil consensus, then our moral, political and economic responsibilities do not stop at the moment of birth. Those who defend the right to life of the weakest among us must be equally visible in support of the quality of life of the powerless among us: the old and the young, the hungry and the homeless, the undocumented immigrant and the unemployed worker. Such a quality of life posture translates into specific political and economic positions on tax policy, employment generation, welfare policy, nutrition and feeding programs, and health care. Consistency means we cannot have it both ways. We cannot urge a compassionate society and vigorous public policy to protect the rights of the unborn and then argue that compassion and significant public programs on behalf of the needy undermine the moral fiber of society or are beyond the proper scope of government responsibility. Right to life and quality of life complement each other in domestic society.

While this was bold and Catholic to the core, the cardinal positioned the teaching in such a way that it was not only religious but also universal so everyone could come closer to an ethic on the sanctity of life. But politicians soon used the principle for their own agendas. Democrats used it to argue against unjust war, capital punishment, and economic oppression, while Republicans co-opted the principle to reinforce their opposition to abortion, euthanasia, and stem-cell research. Few moved toward the center. They could understand their preconceptions, but consistency was less comprehensible, just as would be Bernardin's gift of peace.

The cardinal knew this was a hard teaching. His desire was to sew the sanctity of life with the quality of life, to defend life and to promote it. He understood the differences but also saw the connections and wanted to build a bridge between pro-life conservatives and social justice liberals. Slowly the idea took root in Catholic consciousness. In 1994 the U.S. Conference of Catholic Bishops endorsed the principle as an alternative to violence. In 1995 Pope John Paul II issued the encyclical *The Gospel of Life*, encouraging "a culture of life" over a "culture of death." He wrote:

> Where life is involved, the service of charity must be profoundly consistent. It cannot tolerate bias and discrimination, for human life is sacred and inviolable at every stage and in every situation: it is an indivisible good. We need then to "show care" for all life and for the life of everyone.

Cardinal Bernardin died in peace in 1996.

The Catholic Church has always based its moral beliefs on the dignity of the human person. The unique contribution of Cardinal Bernardin was to weave the disparate threads into a whole cloth. The result has been increased clarity in church teachings about modern warfare, abortion, capital punishment, genetics, and care for the terminally ill. It is still not an easy teaching, but for the first time in a long time there are fewer "single issue" Catholics and more who think twice—and three times—about contemporary moral dilemmas. Thanks to more comprehensive education on life-and-death issues, most people are no longer on the far left or far right of these matters but are sitting squarely on the middle of the fence, an uncomfortable but honest place to be. More and more, people are seeing the unity of life and their responsibility not to rip it apart as the soldiers did Christ's garments, but to keep it whole.

I'm still Catholic because the church has a consistent ethic of life. The seamless garment is not always comfortable, but it fits all sizes.

20

The Church's Best-Kept Secret

I beg you, look for the words "social justice" or "economic justice" on your church website. If you find it, run as fast as you can. Social justice and economic justice, they are code words. Now, am I advising people to leave their church? Yes!
—GLENN BECK, MARCH 2, 2010

Now the whole group of those who believed were of one heart and soul, and no one claimed private ownership of any possessions, but everything they owned was held in common. . . . There was not a needy person among them, for as many as owned lands or houses sold them and brought the proceeds of what was sold. They laid it at the apostles' feet, and it was distributed to each as any had need.
—ACTS OF THE APOSTLES 4:32–35, CIRCA 112

The difference between communism and Christianity? Communism says you must be good. Christianity says it's good to be good.

Catholic social thought is not political but spiritual. It springs from the knowledge that each of us is made in the image and likeness of God. Just as a sunbeam cannot be separated from the sun or any other sunbeam, none of us can be separated from God or any other human being. We are all radiances of one light.

Catholic social teaching is founded on the principle of solidarity: a spiritual awareness that each of us is responsible for the good of all of us. It is knowing that when a family in Chicago gets food stamps, a city is richer; when a family in Maine receives health care, a state is healthier; when taxes from a corporation in Manhattan help provide shelter for a homeless family on the Gulf Coast, a country is stronger; and when a wealthy country sends AIDS medicine to families in Nigeria, the entire world is blessed.

Catholic social thought traces back to the Old Testament, but its official teachings date back to the time of Oliver Twist, who got into trouble for asking, "Please, sir, may I have some more?" That was the best of times and the worst of times, a time of liberating wealth and suffocating poverty, a time of robber barons and child laborers. In 1891 Pope Leo XIII wrote his historic encyclical *Rerum Novarum (The Condition of Labor)*, which addressed social and economic injustice:

> Let it be taken for granted that workman and employer should, as a rule, make free agreements, and in particular should agree freely as to wages; nevertheless, there is a dictate of natural justice more imperious and

ancient than any bargain between man and man, that remuneration should be sufficient to maintain the wage-earner in reasonable and frugal comfort. If through necessity or fear of a worse evil the workman accept harder conditions because an employer or contractor will afford him no better, he is made the victim of force and injustice.

The encyclical also criticizes the socialism of Karl Marx and defends the right to own private property. Mr. Beck would applaud it.

What has always disturbed critics is that the encyclical, and all the teachings of the church on these issues, put responsibility not only on individuals but also on institutions—economic, political, and social. The church teaches that human beings have a fundamental right to life, food, shelter, health care, education, and employment, and that government has a moral responsibility to support these rights. The Catholic principle of subsidiarity holds that when basic needs are not being met at the grassroots level, then it is not only necessary but imperative that government, first local, then state and federal, do what it can to help. The church doesn't tell the state what its public policies or technical solutions should be; it simply does what it is meant to do: offer moral challenges that flow from its spiritual vision: "When I was hungry you gave me something to eat, when I was thirsty you gave me something to drink, when I was a stranger you invited me in, when I needed clothes you clothed me, when I was sick you looked after me, and when I was in prison you came to visit me. I tell you the truth: whatever you do for the least of these my brethren you do for me" (Matthew 25:30–41, NIV).

> As followers of Christ, we are challenged to make a fundamental "option for the poor"–to speak for the voiceless, to defend the defenseless, to assess life styles, policies, and social institutions in terms of their impact on the poor. This "option for the poor" does not mean pitting one group against another, but rather, strengthening the whole community by assisting those who are the most vulnerable. As Christians, we are called to respond to the needs of all our brothers and sisters, but those with the greatest needs require the greatest response.
>
> —ECONOMIC JUSTICE FOR ALL: PASTORAL LETTER ON CATHOLIC SOCIAL TEACHING AND THE U.S. ECONOMY, U.S. BISHOPS, 1986

Since *Rerum Novarum* in 1891, the Catholic Church has issued numerous documents and statements on social and economic justice. The issues have expanded to include religious freedom, the environment, immigration, modern warfare, and torture. Running throughout everything is a primary concern for the poor and vulnerable.

The church in its teachings endeavors to have, or put on, the mind of Christ (1 Corinthians 2:16). Jesus was born in a stable. His parents were refugees. He lived among the poor, fed multitudes with the only food available, was friendly with the rich and the marginal and brought them together, and when he died his only possession was a seamless garment. The only valid criticism of the church is not that its social teachings go too far but that it doesn't always practice what it teaches.

The chosen part is clear. Mother Teresa expressed it by her life and in her simple words: "Whoever the poorest of the poor are, they are Christ for us—Christ under the guise of human suffering." If you see the words "social justice" or "economic justice" on a sign in front of your church, you can know it is pointing in the right direction.

Catholic Social Teaching, according to the Orbis book of the same name, is "our best-kept secret." It's a secret because nobody wants to hear about it. I'm still Catholic because it challenges me to be a better Christian.

21

Everyone Has a Guardian Angel

*Look, Daddy. Teacher says, every time a bell rings
an angel gets his wings!*
—ZUZU BAILEY, IT'S A WONDERFUL LIFE

I believe in angels.
—ABBA, "I HAVE A DREAM"

In a 2007 Gallup poll, three out of four Americans said, "I believe in angels." Americans trust angels ten times more than they do their congressmen. That makes sense.

Angels are a traditional Catholic idea, but how well do we understand what we believe in? How many of us think of angels as heavenly Tinkerbells? It never hurts to be like Zuzu Bailey and, when we take our favorite ornament out of the box, polish it and hold it in front of our eyes before placing it on the tree. We may see something new. Does an angel really get its wings every time a Christmas bell rings?

Of course it does!

Now on to the next question. What is an angel? An angel is a messenger from God.

Like the UPS man?

No, an angel is more like the postman. But unlike a postman in Alabama, say, who delivers a letter from Alaska to a third person in Mobile, the angelic messenger and its message are *one*. An angel is a good idea from God.

The message comes from God to a child of God, just like that. That's why we can't see angels. They're instant.

"An angel gives us a closer idea of God," writes Meister Eckhart. "That is all an angel is: an idea of God."

The bible story of Abraham and Isaac suggests how it works, and maybe doesn't work. Abraham was the father of the Israelites and had a beloved son named Isaac who was his heir. Abraham thought he heard an angel of God telling him to sacrifice Isaac. In those days people believed they would please God by killing people for God because God was still angry with Adam and Eve. So Abraham took his son to a far place, bound him on an altar, put a knife to his throat, and then heard a stronger message: "Abraham! Abraham! Do not lay a hand on the boy. Do not do anything to him!" That voice was the real angel.

Then Abraham heard the first voice again: "Now I know that you fear God because you have not withheld from me your son, your only son." That may have been the voice of human guilt getting in the last word. So Abraham went and sacrificed a ram.

That was the most momentous turning point in religious history since Adam's son Cain killed his brother, Abel. It marked the beginning of the end to human sacrifice.

Centuries later the same angel assured the psalmist that God does not delight in sacrifice or is pleased with burnt offerings (Psalm 51:16). And centuries after that the Son of God would willingly lay down his life for all of us and rise from the dead to prove that everything he taught was true. Before his death Jesus said: "If you had known what this means, 'I desire mercy and not sacrifice,' you would not have condemned the guiltless" (Matthew 12:7).

Jesus' death was the most momentous turning point in all history. It was a lesson so profound that no one could look at sacrificial scapegoating of an innocent victim in the same way ever again.

We know today that God does not want us to sacrifice our children. Or anybody else's children. Or even a ram. God desires only good. And he tells us through angels.

But we don't always hear them. The alarming voices of human history drown out "the still, small voice" (1 Kings 19:12, KJV). Some of us still haven't heard the angel's message to Abraham or learned the lesson of Jesus' sacrifice, and we commit "little murders" all our lives. Sometimes we hear mixed messages, as it appears Abraham did, and become "double-minded, and unstable in every way" (James 1:8, NRSV). We need to discern the good ideas from God beneath the static of fear, anger, and guilt. We know the message is an angel only when it has the qualities of the Sender, not of mere human nature. If the idea brings love and peace, as the second did to Abraham, we know it has found the right address. St. Ignatius of Loyola teaches us how to recognize God's messages: "The action of the good angel is delicate, gentle, delightful. It may be compared to a drop of water penetrating a sponge. The action of the evil spirit upon such souls is violent, noisy, and disturbing. It may be compared to a drop of water falling upon a stone." (*The Spiritual Exercises of St. Ignatius,* #335, Puhl trans.)

Catholicism says we are surrounded by angels—God's blessed ideas for us—just as surely as if we were in the center of a fresco painted by Raphael. Angels guided Mary and Joseph on their flight from Bethlehem to Egypt. Angels guarded Jesus in the desert and comforted him in the Garden of Gethsemane. Jesus counseled all of us: "See that you never look down upon one of these children, for I say to you that their angels in heaven always see the face of my Father who is in heaven" (Matthew 18:10, adapted). Was he not telling us that children see the face of God more clearly than adults because they are open to visits from angels? "Angels," writes Richard McBrien in *Catholicism,* "are reminders that there is more to the created order than what we actually see, feel, hear, and taste."

To be open to angels is to be open to miracles. A miracle is an angel heard.

I'm still Catholic because I learned in Catholic school that I have a guardian angel. That was a small but significant turning point in my history. You know, I haven't said the following prayer in a long, long time, but I think I will now. It is the first prayer I ever learned.

Angel of God, my guardian dear
to whom God's love commits me here.
Ever this day be at my side
to light and guard, to rule and guide.
Amen.

22

Benedicamus Domino!
or, Catholics Like to Party

Wherever the Catholic sun doth shine,
There's always laughter and good red wine.
At least I've always found it so.
Benedicamus Domino!

—HILAIRE BELLOC

Have you ever been to an Irish wake? An Italian wedding? Polka night at St. Stanislaus Kostka parish in Chicago? Oktoberfest in Milwaukee? Have you ever sung and swayed with the gospel choir at Holy Name of Jesus Church in Los Angeles? Taken your kids to the Carnival of Fun at St. Catherine of Sienna in Riverside, Connecticut? Celebrated being alive during the three-week fiesta in San Antonio? If you're frustrated with the Catholic Church, maybe you need to get around more.

Catholicism is an ethnic religion, a coat of many colors, a kaleidoscope in which dazzling pieces of colored glass keep turning to the light and meeting at the center. It's a religion of pipe organs and concertinas, kettle drums and bongos, triangles and trombones. You can smell freshly baked bread or sizzling sausage or good old American hamburgers at any old Catholic picnic or bake sale or feast in any old Catholic parish on any old summer night of the year. Catholics like to get together and eat cholesterol and drink beer and have fun with friends. It's a Jesus thing.

Jesus palled around with people who liked to have fun. His first miracle was turning water into wine at a wedding party. The people who didn't like him called him a glutton and a drunkard because he associated with sinners (Matthew 11:18). Do you think the Last Supper was a somber affair? It was a going-away party at which Jesus gave the whole world an everlasting gift. And when he rose from the dead and met two of his friends who didn't recognize him, he said, "Let's eat." They recognized him in the breaking of the bread. Can you imagine how heartily Jesus must have laughed?

The saints liked to party too. St. Brigid, God bless her Irish soul, said: "I would like a great lake of beer for the King of kings. I would like to be watching heaven's family drinking it through all eternity." St. Teresa of Ávila prayed, "From silly devotions and sour-faced saints, good Lord, deliver us!" The greatest Catholic host may have been Angelo Roncalli (1881–1963), aka Pope John XXIII, who threw a party for the whole church called Vatican II. He opened the windows and beautiful doves flew in and angels flew out from the hidden deposit of faith. It was a party of ideas, a celebration of the chosen part of things.

Here was a man who knew what was real. Jean Maalouf in his book *Pope John XXIII: Essential Writings* tells this story:

> A few days after his coronation John held a special audience for his family, a privilege granted to each new occupant of St. Peter's Chair. The Roncallis entered the apartments in the apostolic palace timidly. The splendor of the place troubled their simple souls. Finally, bashful and confused, they stood before the white-clad figure of the pope. In their confusion they dropped their little presents. Peasant bread, ham, and wine, packed in brightly colored handkerchiefs, all tumbled to the floor. John looked at their staring eyes and open mouths. Although the comedy of the situation did not escape him, he spoke reassuringly: "Don't be afraid. It's only me."

That's pretty much what Jesus said after his death when he suddenly appeared to the disciples trembling in the upper room (John 20:19). Jesus loved his friends, had good times with them, and taught them not only how to die but how to live.

If Catholics have always liked to party, the best is yet to come. Joy is infusing the Catholic Church in the

> I am about to create new heavens and a new earth.
> —Isaiah 65:17, NRSV

United States with the emergence of Hispanic Catholics

from Mexico, Puerto Rico, Central and South America. Hispanics/Latinos(as) have contributed 71 percent of the growth of the Church since 1960. More than half the Catholics in the United States under age twenty-five are of Hispanic descent, as are 25 percent of all laypeople engaged in diocesan ministry programs. It's time to take out our most colorful clothes and get ready to salivate at the next church picnic where Italian sausage, American hamburgers, and German lager will be joined by tacos, enchiladas, and burritos. Hispanic Americans, just like the immigrants of the early twentieth century, are bringing something new and rich to the church of the early twenty-first century—and it's not just great food.

A few years ago, the late Fr. Virgil Elizondo, who was both a pastor in San Antonio and a professor at Notre Dame, asked his American quilt of friends, "When are you the happiest?" The responses revealed an interesting difference between U.S.A. Americans and Mexican Americans. He wrote in his book-in-progress, *Why Mexico Matters*:

> For the most part, U.S.A. Americans responded with an "I" answer such as when I am doing good for others, when I have achieved my goal, when I have paid all my credit cards, when I go fishing, golfing, or skiing, when I am home after work drinking a beer and watching a good ball game, when I get a good bonus and so on. With the Mexican Americans the responses were generally in the "We" such as during a family celebration, when we are playing a good

soccer game, enjoying a good meal with friends, at home with the family when the kids are not crying and hollering. In short it seems that for U.S.A. Americans happiness exists in the individual while for the Mexican it exists in the togetherness. One emphasizes the individual while the other emphasizes the relationship.

This is one of the chosen parts of things. Community. Togetherness. Oneness. Just what the party needs.

I'm going to stick around in the church because a new *abrazo* is coming. I wish I could stick around to the beginning of the twenty-second century. Who knows what *la familia* will look like then? One thing is certain. It will throw a party.

23

God Is Found among the Pots and Pans

Work is love made visible.
—Khalil Gibran

God lives also among the pots and pans.
—St. Teresa of Ávila

Artie and I were now in our forties. We had both left the priesthood to marry years ago. Artie was the funniest guy I'd ever known, but here we were drinking beer and sharing memories and he was sad. "You're so lucky," he said. "You have a good job. You edit books with big ideas. You hang around with brains. You even know Edward Schillebeeckx, for crissakes! And here I am, selling toilet paper to Greek restaurants. . . ."

"Artie," I said, "at least people *use* your paper. My books just sit there."

We ordered a pitcher.

Artie didn't know that I was frustrated too. "I don't make enough money either, Art, and people drive me crazy sometimes too. I once asked my publicity director who her favorite author was. She said, 'Albert Camus.' I said, 'But he's dead.' She said, 'Exactly.'"

"The only thing I know how to do well," Artie said, "is to be a priest." Truth was, Artie could do everything well. But his happiest work moments were as a priest. He was one of the best.

Is there such a thing as finding joy in our job no matter what it is? Is one kind of work inherently more fulfilling than another? Or is it our job to bring joy to whatever we do?

"The kind of work we do does not make us holy," wrote Meister Eckhart, "but we may make it holy."

So I look at the saints and wonder if we folks in the twenty-first century can still be like them. Can we be like St. Teresa in the sixteenth century, who found God among the pots and pans, or Brother Lawrence in the seventeenth who looked at his kitchen and saw a chapel, or Thérèse of Lisieux in the nineteenth who said (before any twentieth-century New Ager), "Each small task of everyday life is part of the total harmony of the universe"? I think we can, sometimes—they did—but not all the time. Nobody's perfect, not even the saints. I love St. Thérèse when she writes in her diary that some of her colleagues drove her nuts.

I also love the Zen story of the two monks carrying empty buckets to the bottom of a hill, where they filled them with water at the stream. They carried the full buckets back up to the monastery, emptied them, and then went back down the hill for more. Up and down, all day long, carrying buckets of water and smiling as if they were walking two feet off the ground. A stranger passing by watched them, puzzled, and asked, "Why are you so happy?" One of the monks answered, "We are bringing buckets of water up to the monastery!"

What makes the difference between working with frustration and working with love?

Love comes when we least expect it, when we no longer identify ourselves with our jobs but lose ourselves in the sacrament of the moment. Suddenly, we are no longer a teacher but teaching, no longer a repairman but repairing, no longer a salesperson but providing, no longer an accountant but balancing, no longer a mom but nurturing, comforting, and healing. Isn't this what makes the difference—the awareness that it is no longer we who are doing the work but the Love within us that does its work (John 14:10)?

It's also important to understand that "we work for money but we live for God" (Thomas Hora). We work for money seven, eight, maybe fourteen hours a day to live a comfortable life and provide for others. We live for God twenty-four hours a day, no matter what our work is.

Catholics somehow got the idea that working for money is unholy even though Jesus said, "The laborer deserves to be paid" (Luke 10:7, NRSV). Many of the saints didn't need to work for money to provide shelter and food and a little bit more for themselves and their families. Many didn't even have spouses or children but lived in monastic communities. That culture is disappearing. If Brother Lawrence were alive today, he might be a chef in a Greek restaurant, and while he would still practice the presence of God, he would also be grateful for his unemployment insurance. If Thérèse of Lisieux were alive today, she might be the most-beloved caregiver in a nursing home, but she would also make sure the home offered health insurance. If Teresa of Ávila were here today, she could well be the president of her own corporation and a philanthropist, but prayer would still be the center of her life. "We work for money, we live for God." They are not mutually exclusive, and if we know what we are here for, we will know how to work.

We may even change our jobs, more than once. Or not.

Which brings us back to Artie and me. Years later, Artie, no longer married, returned to the priesthood. With his son.

I remember his first phone call from the rectory. "Hold on a second," he said. I heard background noise. "Place is going nuts," he said. "I've got the mover here and he's saying, 'Mister, sign this!' My son is yelling, 'Dad!' And the secretary says someone wants to see Father. This is going to be fun!"

On my fiftieth birthday Vickie and our two sons threw a surprise party for me. My dad, my hero, flew in from Chicago to surprise me. Friends and loved ones filled our house. They asked me to give a speech. I said, "I think I finally know what I want to be when I grow up. What I am right now."

I don't always love doing what I do but that's because I'm still discovering who and what I really am and what I'm here for. I know the words. I'm learning the Answer.

24

The Papacy, or It's a Tough Job but Somebody's Got to Do It

It often happens that I wake up at night and begin to think about a serious problem and decide I must tell the Pope about it. Then I wake up completely and remember that I am the pope.
—POPE JOHN XXIII (1881–1963)

In the movie *Manhattan* Woody Allen advises a friend to do the right thing. His friend says, "You are so self-righteous. I mean, we're just people. We're just human beings. You think you're God!"

Allen shrugs and says, "I gotta model myself after *someone.*"

We all need role models. God is the best. It also helps to have role models in the world who remind us to do the right thing. When it works, the papacy does a good job of that.

Who doesn't remember Pope John Paul II cooing love syllables with the young people at Madison Square Garden and defeating communism in Poland with quiet diplomacy? How moved we all were when Pope Francis embraced and kissed the face of the severely disfigured man suffering from "Elephant Man's" disease. Who can ever forget "Good Pope John," who before becoming John XXIII helped save thousands of Jews from the Nazis and later opened the windows of the church as if they were eyes taking in the world for the first time. You probably don't know Pope Gregory the Great (c. 540–604), but when the hierarchy was even less credible than it is today, he insisted that bishops be first and foremost "physicians of the soul" and order their lives from a spiritual point of view. Gregory was also the first pope to refer to himself not as "Supreme Pontiff" or "His Holiness" but as "servant of the servants of God." Gregory, John, and John Paul—they all knew: "Whosoever will be chief among you, let him be your servant" (Matthew 20:27, KJV).

Not all 265 popes since Peter were role models. The papacy is like a net of fish: you never know what you're going to catch. In Morris West's novel *Lazarus* a character muses about the history of the popes: "Saints and sinners, wise men and fools, ruffians, rogues, reformers, and even an occasional madman! When they are gone, they are added to the list which began with Peter the Fisherman. The good are venerated; the bad are ignored. But the Church goes on."

Indeed it does, and let's face it: most people today don't know anything about anybody, good or bad, who hasn't been famous during the past three days (cf. Jay Leno, Jaywalking). Take the bad popes (please). Does anyone remember Pope Paul III (1468–1549), who murdered his mother for her inheritance, resolved a theological dispute between bishops by having them hacked to death, and took over the prostitution business so he could get a piece of the pie? Now there's a man who knew how to balance a budget. Do you know who the second pope was? His name was Linus, and he didn't drag around a blankie; that was another Linus. Truth is, most Americans wouldn't know that John Adams was the second president if it weren't for HBO. Do you know who Paul Giamatti is? You're ahead of the curve.

When the topic of the papacy comes up for academic debate, the key issue is whether or not the pope is infallible. One person says, "All the popes are descended from Peter, who was given the keys to the kingdom of heaven, and that is why they are infallible." Another responds, "Only God is infallible." They usually don't have much to say after that. Truth is, the doctrine of infallibility wasn't even declared until 1870 at the First Vatican Council, and it has conditions attached to it under the rubric of *ex cathedra*, which renders it rare at best. Since 1870 there has been only *one* infallible statement *ex cathedra*: the Assumption of Mary in 1950, and one declared *ex cathedra in retro*, the Immaculate Conception in 1854. Catholics celebrate the Feast of the Immaculate Conception every December 8th and, if you are an average Catholic, chances are fifty-fifty that you know what it means. It refers not to the conception of Jesus but to the conception of Mary.

The issue of infallibility is not a topic of interest for Catholics. No one goes to bed at night worrying about it. It rarely comes up in conversations. What comes up are the same kinds of questions people pose about all religious leaders: "How is he doing? Is he a holy man? What is he doing to help us want to be more like Christ and love our neighbors as ourselves?"

The pope represents 1.3 billion Catholics. The whole world is interested in what he says and does. Basketball star LeBron James gets less attention. It's a tough job, but somebody's got to do it.

And when it works, it's so beautiful. When John Paul II, seeking to heal centuries of misunderstanding between Christians and Jews, visited Auschwitz and became the first pope to pray in a synagogue, he began a new chapter in religious history. When Paul VI went to the United Nations in the midst of the Vietnam War to declare, "No more war, war never again! One cannot love with offensive weapons in his hands!" he challenged every world leader to seek peace. When Pius XII during World War II helped save more than eight hundred thousand Jews from death through public appeals, hidden sanctuaries, ransom monies, emergency passports, fake baptismal certificates, and diplomatic maneuverings—despite his critics' claims that he should have done more—he fulfilled the Talmud injunction "Whoever saves a life, it is considered as if he saved an entire world!"

That's what a pope is: the servant of the servants of God. It is a wonderful job.

And—did you know this?—any Catholic can be elected pope.

Back in 2005, as the cardinals were soon to elect a pope to follow John Paul II, the e-zine *Just Good Company*, just for good fun, asked me to write a brief essay on what

I would do if I were pope. I wrote it in one fell swoop and was amazed to see it go viral throughout the U.S. and as far as Europe and Australia. I include it now just in case a lot of cardinals read this book and are so taken by it they'd like to send my name up in white smoke the next time. I'm only seventy; it could happen.

If I were Pope I'd have a ball. I'd be "Happy Pope," and smile a lot. I'd stand on the balcony and stretch out my arms in a great embrace and tell everyone I love them and, even better, God loves them, no matter what. I'd tell everybody wherever I went that nothing can separate them from the love of God, not death, not sin, not anyone or anything. I'd tell that to my worker bees in the Curia before reducing it by half and encouraging every priest under sixty to join the missions. I'd tell that to sinners, saints, and fools, to liberals, conservatives, and confused, to Catholics, Protestants, Muslims, and Jews. I'd preach God's unconditional love to God's children in every country, to those with AIDS in Africa, to those in prisons and in hospitals, to those who are divorced and remarried, to everybody everywhere. They would know that I meant it, and that it was true, even if it was hard for them to believe. Someday, if I said it well enough and often enough, and most of all proved it with my life, other leaders in the church would do it too, and the children of God wouldn't have to believe—they would know. I can't wait to be Pope! I'll live in the Vatican two months a year to catch up on paperwork, but the rest of the year I'll live in parishes throughout the world—the one by Cabrini Green in Chicago, the one under suspicion in Beijing, the one high in the Alto Plano of Peru. I'll be like Henry Fonda in *The Grapes of Wrath*: "A fellow ain't got a soul of his own, just a little piece of a big soul, the one big soul that belongs to everybody, so I'll be everywhere, wherever you can look. Wherever there's a fight so hungry people can eat, I'll be there. Wherever there's a cop beatin' up a guy, I'll be there. I'll be in the way guys yell when they're mad. I'll be in the way kids laugh when they're hungry and they know supper's ready, and where people are eatin' the stuff they raise and livin' in the houses they build. I'll be there too!" Yup, that's where I'll be when I'm Pope. I'll be in Israel and Palestine, in Bosnia and Afghanistan; I'll sleep in a favela in Brazil, a high-rise in Manhattan, and a houseboat in the bay of Hong Kong. And wherever I am, I'll preach nothing more and nothing less than the incredible, overwhelming love of God that is closer to us than breathing, and nearer than hands and feet. I'd like to write more about when I'm Pope but I've got to go now and practice my embrace. The way I see it, even if I don't get to be Pope, it's important to become that kind of person wherever and whatever I happen to be.

Little did I know that eight years later, Pope Francis would come along and be all that and more.

25

The Best Is Yet to Come

*No eye has seen, no ear has heard, and no
mind has imagined the things that God has
prepared for those who love him.*
—1 CORINTHIANS 2:9, GOD'S WORD TRANSLATION

See, I am making all things new.
—REVELATION 21:5, NRSV

You ain't seen nuthin' yet!
—JIMMY DURANTE

When Vickie and I first met, I asked her, "What is your philosophy of life?" She said without hesitation, "Life is for shit."

"How can you say that?" I said. "You're a happy, cheerful person."

"You see my eye," she said. Her right eye was scarred and cloudy, the color of a sea shell. When she was fifteen months old, Vickie fell on a glass Easter rabbit and was blinded in that eye. "When I was a little girl, I walked with my face down so people wouldn't see how ugly I was.

Sometimes people, even strangers, asked me embarrassing questions or made hurtful remarks. When the kids played games, I was always the monster. I grew up imagining that everyone looked at me with disdain, as if the way I looked was my fault. I was a freak. Life was for shit. Thank God there was a heaven at the end."

"How did you get through the days?"

"Mama. She always said to me, 'Hold your head up high and face the world.' It became a litany that became a part of me. She would hold me in her arms and stroke my hair and say, 'If you hold your head up high, it will be okay, and people will see your beautiful soul.' She said it again and again. She said it whenever I wanted to hide. When I was in high school, I was popular and got all A's. I was even elected class president, but I still felt like a freak. All I wanted was to look like everybody else. When things got really bad, I would cry to Mama, and she would look at me with her loving eyes and say, 'Hold your head up high and face the world. Let them see the beauty inside.'"

I told her the truth: she was just as beautiful on the *outside.*

She knew I meant it. "What is your philosophy of life?" she asked.

"That heaven begins right here. We couldn't be further apart. Yet I walk around with a sadness in my heart. And you walk around glowing, with your head held high. What gives?"

One year later we were married.

A month after we wed, Vickie's bad eye got infected. It had to be removed. She received an artificial eye that was soft and green, just like her good one. She now looked like everybody else.

Forty-one years later Vickie still believes that life is for shit, but she also knows that heaven does begin right here. I still believe that heaven begins right here but have also come to accept that life is for shit. We both walk with our heads held high and smile a lot.

Both sides are true.

Catholicism promises us that after we die we will see Beauty that eyes cannot see. We will hear Music that ears cannot hear. We will know Love that no mind can imagine.

And it all begins right here, on the spot where we are standing. Like Moses and Isaiah, whether we know it or not, "we are standing on holy ground" (Exodus 3:5).

Life on earth is hard and often cruel, but—thank God—God is not only Abba (Daddy) but Mama and Mamma Lou, caressing us, comforting us, holding us, telling us how beautiful we are, no matter how things look or what people think. When Jesus looked over the city of Jerusalem, he said, "How often have I wanted to gather your children as a mother hen gathers her brood under her wings!" Pope John Paul II compared God's love to the love that only a mother can give: "tender, merciful, patient, and full of understanding." When life on earth is for shit, and it often is, God hugs us and holds us in her arms and inspires us to hold our head up high. And she promises to make all things new.

Vickie and I talk about heaven sometimes, and again we couldn't be further apart. I think what is good and beautiful and true in us continues without interruption, but I can't imagine what it is like. Vickie is specific. She envisions a beatific vision that is like being in a great big show with all your loved ones and watching a movie on a huge screen.

"But that would be boring," I tell her.

"No," she assures me. "It's the beatific vision."

So I ask her, "Okay, if you get there first, order a big recliner for me. I can already see Mama Lou on her big blue sofa and Mama next to you in her big easy chair and you on a comfy overstuffed chair too, but I see a hard folding chair on your right waiting for me. Please ask God for a recliner, like the one in the family room, okay?"

"I will."

Nobody knows what life after death will be like. But I know it will be.

I am still Catholic because heaven makes perfect sense.

A Six-Week Discussion Guide
for *Positively Catholic*

Week One: Chapters 1–4

1. What sacraments with a small *s* have you received recently?

2. What sacraments with a small *s* have you given recently?

3. How does your understanding and experience of God change when you consider an "elsewhere God" as opposed to an "everywhere God"?

4. Can you share about a time when God found you in "the sacrament of the present moment"?

5. It's easy to understand the words "nothing can separate us from the love of God," but in practice, what does that sentiment really mean to you? How would you apply it to people—of all sorts—you know?

Week Two: Chapters 5–9

1. How can "doing good to feel good" lead us into trouble?

2. Can you give your own explanation of why bad things happen to good people? How do you react to the phrase *redemptive suffering*?

3. What is the difference between knowing about God and knowing God? Can you describe a way of knowing that is not directly rational, or related to the brain? What difference does this make?

4. How different might the world be if everyone understood and believed that we are all, Christian or non-Christian, members of the mystical body of Christ?

5. What is your relationship like with Mary, the mother of God? Do you believe that you can go to God through her? Do you have any experiences of this that you would like to share?

Week Three: Chapters 10–13

1. What is your Catholic story?

2. Do you carry the sense that your own sins helped nail Jesus to the cross? How does the answer to that question shape your idea of who and what God is?

3. How have you seen the church change in your lifetime?

4. In what ways do you think the church might change over the next ten years? The next hundred years?

5. How do you feel about chapter 13's statement: "You Can Disagree with the Church and Still Be a Good Catholic"? What kind of experience have you had with this concept?

Week Four: Chapters 14–17

1. Describe the Bethlehem Principle in your own words. Do you believe it is true? Why or why not?

2. What is your favorite image of church?

3. Spend some time thinking about how Leach describes the Eucharist in chapter 16. What does the Eucharist mean to you?

4. Have you explored any of the spiritual paths of the different religious orders? If so, how have they spoken to you?

5. Which Catholic spiritual traditions or practices nurture you most? Have you ever found your Catholic faith enriched by another religious tradition?

Week Five: Chapters 18–21

1. Have you ever applied the fruits of the spirit as a test to determine if something is spiritually valid in your life? How might your life change if you weighed whether or not something brings you love, peace, patience, kindness, goodness, faithfulness, gentleness, and/or discipline?

2. How does the suffering of a child in Calcutta affect a child in California?

3. Reread Cardinal Bernardin's explanation of the Seamless Garment of Life in chapter 19. Spend some time thinking about this concept. How might

this principle change our society if more people understood and embraced it?

4. How do you see the economic, political, and social institutions of society bearing responsibility for the common good? How might that responsibility manifest itself?

5. How open are you to angels? Have you experienced any kind of angelic presence or intervention you would be willing to talk about?

Week Six: Chapters 22–25

1. In what ways has your Catholic faith been a party? How has community been a part of that?

2. How is God "among the pots and pans" of your daily work?

3. Are "working for money" and "living for God" compatible concepts? Is it possible to be financially successful and holy?

4. What would you do if you were pope?

5. What does it mean, to you, to say that "heaven begins right here"?

About the Author

MICHAEL LEACH is publisher emeritus and editor-at-large of Orbis Books. A leader in Catholic publishing for thirty years, he has edited and published more than three thousand books. His authors include Nobel Prize winners, National Book Award winners, and hundreds of Catholic Book Award winners. He has served as president of the Catholic Book Publishers Association and the ecumenical Religion Publishers Group. Before joining Orbis as publisher in 1997 he was president of the Crossroad Publishing Company in New York City. In 2007 the Catholic Book Publishers Association honored him with a Lifetime Achievement Award. Dubbed "the dean of Catholic book publishing" by *U.S. Catholic* magazine, he has authored or edited several books of his own, including the bestseller *I Like Being Catholic* and *A Maryknoll Book of Prayer, The People's Catechism*, and *I Like Being Married*. A popular speaker at conferences nationwide, Michael lives in Connecticut with Vickie, his wife of forty-eight years.